FIRING

GW01445022

FIRING DAYS
AT
SALTLEY

TERRY ESSERY

D. BRADFORD BARTON

ISBN 0 85153 375 2

first published by
D. BRADFORD BARTON LIMITED
TRURO · CORNWALL
© **TERRY ESSERY**

printed in Great Britain by
LOVELL BAINES PRINT LTD · NEWBURY · BERKSHIRE

CONTENTS

INTRODUCTION

It was the evening of one of those perfect days in early summer which unfortunately bless these Islands only too rarely. Two small boys wearing coats over their pyjamas crept downstairs, quietly unlatched the side door and scuttled the few yards from their front garden to a lineside fence. Climbing on the top rail, they perched with ears cocked, listening for the first rumble of an approaching express. This operation was performed as often as circumstances would allow, since the 7.00 p.m. express from Worcester to Birmingham was the highlight of the day's 'spotting' on that section of ex-G.W.R. track which winds its way through Shirley, Hall Green and Tyseley to Snow Hill station.

That first faint rumble, carried on the still air, rapidly grew to that once-familiar pounding roar which only a steam locomotive can produce. The two boys bounced up and down in excited anticipation as a gleaming 'Saint' - 'Lady of the Lake' - exploded into view. A fleeting glimpse of flashing side rods, a friendly nod from an imperious driver, the pink tinge of fire on steam matching the glow in the western sky, the glorious crescendo of sound and then all was gone. The boys lingered a while, listening to the fading sound of wheels on rails, before quickly dashing home to the side door and swiftly sneaking back to bed to dream their own individual dreams of railways in general and locomotives in particular. It never seriously occurred to either of them in those days just before Hitler's machinations set Europe ablaze, that both would in time spend their early working days with British Railways and that the younger would indeed fire and, at times, drive over that particular section of track.

It was hardly surprising therefore that, living alongside the Worcester - Birmingham line, both boys were badly bitten by the 'Railway Bug' at an early age. These two youngsters belonged to a group of lads who showed a great enthusiasm for train spotting, and they travelled to as many vantage points as their limited pocket money in those austerity war years would allow. There were many such places in and around Birmingham, and interest was equally divided between the G.W.R. and L.M.S.

As the younger brother of the 'two', I must admit that

I did not at first relish the hours spent on cold, dirty
station platforms or bleak wind-swept bridges. I merely
'tagged along' with my elders so as not to be left out of
things. However, my fondness for the G.W. grew one day
at Snow Hill station when I was first invited on to the
footplate of a 'Hall'.

As a youngster, my blond hair, blue eyes and innocent
expression quickly melted the heart of even the sternest
of the old school of engine drivers. My ability to 'cab'
engines became almost legendary in our circle of friends.
I believe it was this early footplate experience, coupled
with a few short rides, that created the desire actually
to handle and master one of these magnificent beasts.

I very much favoured the Great Western in those days,
mostly because their crews seemed friendlier, allowing me
to 'cab' more engines, and both stations and locomotives
were very much cleaner. The old 'Duke' Class were my
great favourites, being so unlike the other G.W. locos.
Their appearance was as noble as their names, with their
large domes, tall chimneys and all a-gleam with shining
copper and brass work. Indeed, the highlight of my
youthful cabbing career was when I finally 'cornered'
'Duke of Cornwall' on Snow Hill station.

Gradually though, interest in the L.M.S. grew,
particularly after a day's 'spotting' at Tamworth watching the 'Duchesses' hurtling past with their heavy loads.
About this time we moved to the Small Heath district of
Birmingham which, by way of coincidence, was located
about halfway between Tyseley and Saltley locomotive
depots, the principal G.W.R. and L.M.S. sheds in the
area. Visits to these on a Sunday afternoon were
memorable indeed and in the spring of 1948 I was
delighted when brother Bob one day announced that he had
signed on as a cleaner at Tyseley motive power depot.
Every day I required a full report on what happened
during his shift, what engines he cleaned and how he did
it. Despite the dirt and obvious hard work, he was
gloriously happy, being a true Western enthusiast, so it
was with some considerable surprise that after a few
weeks he told me that he had transferred to Saltley. A
friend of his had done this some six weeks earlier and
was now enjoying firing turns as a Passed Cleaner.
This then was the incentive, to be Passed Out in six to
eight weeks, even if on an 'inferior' railway.

After this event, our interest and enthusiasm for the
L.M.S. developed, and has remained ever since. I was
envious of my brother's adventures and details of these

only served to whet my appetite. He was quickly out firing and had acquired quite a bit of main line experience before being rounded up to serve his King and Country for eighteen months.

In the meantime, I was straining at the leash. Being nearly three years his junior the waiting seemed interminable, and it was therefore with great excitement that one day in February 1950, at the age of sixteen, I signed on at Saltley as a cleaner.

I
SALTLEY SHED

Saltley shed owed its existence to the need for the old Midland Railway to have a stable in the heart of the great rail complex which was interwoven throughout the Birmingham industrial connurbation. Such a stable should ideally be adjacent to their Derby to Bristol artery, and in this respect Saltley's location was near perfect, being only a short stone's throw from these illustrious if somewhat grimy tracks.

It was primarily required to supply freight engines for the numerous local workings involved in collecting and distributing the immense amount of industrial and other merchandise moving in the area. This traffic, having been concentrated and sorted in the major marshalling yards of Lawley Street, Washwood Heath, Bromford and Water Orton, had to be shipped farther afield and suitable motive power also had to be provided. Though freight working was the major concern of Saltley, passenger engines were required too, but these were geared to the commuter traffic of the district rather than expresses.

Geographically speaking, Birmingham is roughly halfway between Bristol and the industrial area of Sheffield with its associated coalfields. It was, therefore, an ideal staging post for changing crews on passenger and faster freight traffic and changing or replenishing locos on the slower through freights. With so much activity, Saltley was obliged to provide a great many extra crews for the extensive amount of relief work necessitated by the control system. This system tended to keep crews operating in their own locality so that excessive hours need not be worked. Obviously this did not always occur as planned, but the link system at Saltley was based loosely on a progressively expanding field of activity commencing with shed and local shunting duties and terminating with the Carlisles.

In order of seniority the links ran thus:

Washwood Heath link: This was concerned principally with the disposal and preparation of engines, with a few odd turns such as marshalling and any local steam shunting duties that remained, thrown in to relieve the monotony.

Newly registered drivers and firemen cut their teeth in this link but the firemen generally only had to endure at the most one full year, often less, since promotion was initially rapid. Drivers on the other hand were obliged to await a vacancy in the Control link and established drivers did not leave B.R. very frequently. It was for them, therefore, often a case of waiting for a man or men (for they generally left in batches) to retire from the senior links, whereupon a general reshuffle would take place. Firemen would move once a year to a different section of the same link and therefore to a different driver unless a vacancy occurred in a senior link, in which case they would be promoted directly into that vacancy irrespective of the time of year. The reason for this was to give firemen as much experience and route knowledge as possible.

Bank Pilot link: This was the next link in the promotion chain for firemen and was ideal for developing their firing prowess, since it could involve quite hard work banking westbound freights over the four miles between Washwood Heath west end and Kings Heath, the summit of Camp Hill bank.

There were six engines allocated for pilot duties, manned by eighteen sets of crews, working three shifts of approximately eight hours, the crews keeping the same engine for a whole week. The engines used were 3F 0-6-0s but occasionally a Class 4F 0-6-0 found itself on this duty, though they were not, however, popular with the men. Long periods of waiting were unavoidable, and since the driver's seating arrangements were very much inferior to a 3F, the drivers objected. Moreover, they did not warm up as quickly as a 3F and were more temperamental steamers, so this upset the firemen.

One advantage of retaining the same engine for a week was that the crews took a much greater interest in its mechanical condition and general appearance. This led to the rumour that if a 3F was getting a bit run-down and frayed around the edges, then seven days on the 'Bank' would certainly restore its condition.

Drivers had to apply for entry into this link and were therefore older men who might be also afflicted with some ailment or minor disability.

Control link: Having gained a reasonable amount of skills in the Bank Pilot link, firemen were then promoted into the Control link. This consisted of about fifty sets of men who had no booked work, only booked times,

and were used by the Control to relieve crews who were
required to work back to their own depots, or men who
were on overtime, etc., etc.

If a driver had an extensive route knowledge, then
some quite interesting work could be had, particularly in
the summer months when extra excursions and specials were
run. Trips to Bristol and Sheffield were not unusual,
while Gloucester, Derby or Leicester were fairly commonplace; even Crewe or Blackpool could be visited if the
driver was an ex-North West man.

However, the bulk of the work was mainly local relief,
which was not particularly exciting and often meant
disposing of the engine on arrival at the shed. Two or
three such operations could be accomplished in an eight
hour shift, but by way of compensation it could be
truthfully said that every day was different.

Special link: This was a senior Control link in which
about 36 sets of men were used to cover booked work, when
the booked crews were off duty or on rest days, holidays,
etc. They also doubled up on Control work when required,
but activity was usually more predictable.

Trip link: Having now gained a variety of experience,
firemen then passed into the Trip link. This consisted
of twelve sets of men covering the various local trips
necessary to concentrate traffic in the major marshalling
yards. It was a pleasant little link enabling firemen to
acquire an intimate knowledge, through constant repeti-
tion, of local operations. Some interesting and obscure
backwaters could be seen on these turns which no other
link allowed. As with the Bank Pilots, drivers applied
for entry into this link and were therefore of a similar
category, i.e., older men often nearing retirement.

Bottom group of road links, known as Link Three,
sections A-H: When the aspiring fireman arrived in this
group he really felt that he was now out of the Baby
Farm. Each section had twelve sets of men, that is to
say, there was eleven weeks of booked work with one set
covering rest days. Therefore each crew completed the
full section once every twelve weeks or four times per
year. Normally firemen would spend twelve months in each
section of the link and then pass to another section with
another driver until finally promoted to Link Two.

For example, a fireman might enter section C - the
Redditch link - in say May 1951. In May 1952 he would
pass into section B, the Little Bristol link, and in May

1953 he would go into section A. Theoretically he could
pass through all the sections in turn, but in practice
promotion would take him into the next group before the
eight years had passed, which was the period necessary to
accomplish this. Drivers stayed in this link until they
either retired or a vacancy occurred in the Link One
group. They could, however, apply for vacancies in the
Bank Pilots, the Trip link or surprisingly Link Two - the
Passenger Group.

Link Two - the Passenger Group: This consisted of
three sections, A, B and C, and were colloquially known
as the Top, Middle and Bottom Passenger links respectively. Each section contained the usual twelve sets of men
and although a normal promotion link for firemen from
Link Three, drivers had to apply for it. The most
plausible explanation for this would seem to be that
generally less hours were worked because passenger trains
ran more punctually than freight trains and, since much
of the passenger work at Saltley could only be regarded
as short distance operations, pay packets at the end of
the week would be lighter than their colleagues' in the
freight links. Of course there were compensations, since
apart from the dubious status image, social activities
could be more accurately planned, more day working
indulged in and, in the case of section A, mileage
bonuses obtained on the runs to Bristol and Sheffield.
There was also another plus, in that far less preparation
and disposal work was required from passenger men.

Link One: Unlike many sheds, Saltley did not regard
passenger work as the top link - this was the domain of
the long-distance freights, of which the Carlisles and
Glasgows were the elite. Again there were eight sections, A to H, and the experienced (for experienced they
now were) firemen went annually into a different section
until they were finally passed out as drivers.
The few remaining lodging jobs at Saltley were to be
found in these links and great efforts were made by the
shed staff to ensure that the finest engines, with the
best quality coal, were allocated to these turns.

II
A CLEANER'S LOT

The function of an engine cleaner should be to clean
engines, and there is really no better way of getting to
know your way around a loco than by starting at the
front buffer beam and working your way aft, along both
sides, then over and under, while at the same time
scraping off layers of filth to see what lies underneath.
Discovering these bits and pieces and finding out their
place in the scheme of things was all part of the training and, despite the obvious dirtiness of the job, most
cleaners were at their happiest doing just this. It
really made their day if one of the steam risers allowed
them to shovel some coal into the firebox or put an
injector on.

The method of cleaning engines was fairly straightforward. From the level of the footplate downwards,
locomotives tended to be covered with a mixture of oil,
soot, coal dust and general dirt. It was, however,
reasonably soft where it was able to soak up a regular
supply of oil but could be literally inches thick. Most
of this was scraped off with a metal 'scraper', the
residue being sloshed with a lump of cotton waste soaked
in paraffin, and then wiped dry. The boilers and cabs
were attacked by a liberal application of paraffin and
then wiped down. Providing that the paintwork underneath
was still in good condition, quite a presentable job
could be made in this way. Unfortunately there were too
many dirty engines and too few cleaners, and the cleaning
foreman usually had to content himself with ensuring that
engine numbers were rendered readable - but of course
this only emphasised the dirtiness of the rest of the
engine. Occasionally some special event would call for
an all-out effort from the cleaning staff to bring a
locomotive up to the required standard. At Saltley, this
would be the most recently 'shopped' Black Five, and
understandably great enthusiasm was generated by all
concerned, for the results were well worth the labour
involved.

However, because of the acute shortage of shed labour-
ers at that time, most cleaners after two or three weeks
found themselves engaged on a variety of jobs. Many of
these were very good as muscle developers but they were
not so good for morale. One had to be very dedicated to

put up with weeks of shovelling ashes out of the disposal
pits, picking up coal spillage, filling up sand bunkers
and unloading stores. However, this made you familiar
with all the operations of a motive power depot and you
certainly got to know your way around the shed.

My artistic aptitude was soon spotted, and I found
myself armed with a $3\frac{1}{2}'$-long L-shaped paint brush, a
gallon pot of black heat-resistant paint and a 'brief' to
transform every rusty-looking Saltley smokebox to a
cherry blossom shine. After this I had to get down to
some really delicate work and whiten the shed and smokebox numbers. As long as I was on, in, or under a loco I
was very content, but then tragedy struck.

This took the form of being 'invited' to join the
office staff in the shed's general office. I have always
had a great aversion to office routine and having not
long left school I was particularly sensitive to it at
this time. I reacted violently at being kept away from
'my' locomotives. After two weeks of continual badgering
I was transferred to the time office. Here at least I
was in contact with enginemen and the more practical side
of administration. During this period, a new firing
inspector was appointed to the shed and our training
started in earnest. Now this was really interesting and
took in theoretical work plus a certain amount of
practical instruction actually on the footplate.

Classes were held in a lecture room set aside for this
purpose at Saltley station. It was also the home of the
mutual improvement group, so popular with senior firemen
preparing for their driving examination, and contained
many excellent models of engine equipment, diagrams, etc.
Although we were overwhelmed with the amount of things to
learn, we spent many very pleasant hours with Mr.Welch.
His pet theory was that even if we could not at first
raise much steam, it was of paramount importance to be
able to keep boilers well filled, so the use and operation of injectors was rammed down our throats every day.
We all acquired a little black book called 'Questions for
Enginemen' and this became our Bible.

To be fair, Mr.Welsh would always try and back up
theory as soon as possible with a practical demonstration. A few minutes on the footplate with only a little
bit of dialogue such as, 'If you does this, you gets
that, and if you gets that you does this,' was much more
effective in getting the various points home. It was
during one of these demonstrations, which took place on
the footplate of a Class 8 standing on one of the outside

roads of the shed, that I saw Mr.Welch dexterously 'fire'
his bowler hat to the left front corner of the firebox.
I was privileged to witness him perform this unusual feat
on two further occasions.

Much of the fireman's art will be already familiar to
readers, and part only of our lectures need be given
here. For example, how to deal with clinker. If this is
allowed to form in large quantities it will block the air
spaces in the grate and prevent the air supply admitted
through the dampers from passing through the fire which
in consequence will become dead, so that the steaming of
the boiler will be affected. In this event it will be
necessary to break up and dislodge the clinker by using
the straight dart to lift it from the firebars and the
pricker to clear out the air spaces in the grate. Incor-
rect firing and mismanagement of the dampers tends to
accelerate the formation of clinker. One also found
that the stop-go type of running most slow freights were
afflicted with in those days - hours of inactivity in a
lay-by, followed by a short spurt along the main line to
the next block - clinkered the fire as much as anything.

The best safeguard is to spread about a bucketful of
broken clean firebrick or limestone over the grate before
the fire is built up during engine preparation. These
materials tend to collect the clinker round themselves as
it forms, and by so doing prevent it from adhering to the
firebars. A large quantity of air is required to ensure
proper combustion and this is drawn in by the blast and
enters the firebox through the dampers, upwards through
the firegrate and also through the firehole door, to the
top of the fire. Most ex-L.M.S. engines have hollow
firehole doors which allow a certain amount of secondary
air to be admitted even when the doors are closed.

It is nearly always necessary to admit air through
both the firehole door and the dampers. The air drawn
through the firegrate is required to maintain the bed of
fire incandescent, whilst the air admitted by the firehole door serves to complete the combustion of the gases
liberated from the glowing coal below. However, all air
admitted to the firebox over and above the quantity
necessary for complete combustion of the coal will pass
through the boiler unchanged except that it will become
heated in its passage. This means that the surplus air
robs useful heat from the fire which could otherwise be
used to produce steam, and furthermore the loss of this
heat from the fire lowers the temperature of the firebox.

If insufficient air is allowed to enter the firebox,

complete combustion of the coal is impossible because
there will not be enough oxygen to combine with all the
carbon in the fuel and some of the carbon will pass
through the tubes unburned, to appear at the chimney in
the form of smoke. There is also the risk that the
carbon consumed will only be burned to carbon monoxide,
and that the hydrocarbon vapours will also escape
unburned from the chimney, giving rise to a serious heat
loss in addition to the production of smoke. How then is
it possible to judge when the correct amount of air is
being admitted to the firebox to give correct combustion?
One method is to set the dampers and firehole door so
that a clear exhaust is obtained, but that when the firehole door is closed very slightly smoke appears at the
chimney. Another method is to adjust the dampers and
firedoor so that there is just a perceptible
discolouration of the exhaust at the chimney. This
method has the advantage that there is something visible
to watch and there is no chance of admitting excess air.
In either case, if combustion is almost perfect, each
shovel of coal fired will be accompanied by a dash of
smoke from the chimney lasting perhaps one or two
seconds.

I must say that as an experienced fireman, I tended
to prefer the second method, and found that I could
accurately determine the state of the fire by watching
the chimney exhaust. I've congratulated myself many
times on placing a single shovel of coal dead on a
target, which would be no larger than a tea-plate and
perhaps 10' from the firehole, with no more visual
information other than the smoke pattern at the chimney.
To be able to do this was particularly important when
firing an engine very lightly. Firing to the chimney
exhaust, however, was rendered somewhat more tricky at
night, when at times it was not possible to see even the
end of the firebox, let alone what shade of grey was
coming out of the chimney. At Saltley we seemed to work
more at night, so other methods had to be adopted. For
me, however, all these skills were many years in the
future, so back to the Saltley station lecture room.

Much has been said and written on the best way of
firing a locomotive, but the official method was known
as Controlled Firing, and this is what we were taught.
Controlled Firing can be described as firing at equal
time intervals; a definite number of shovels of coal
well broken-up fired at short regular intervals, and the
time between firings not altered by reason of speed or

gradient. The actual number of shovels of coal fired of
course depended on the work the engine had to do and this
had to be determined by experience. Controlled Firing
saved coal because it was never added at such a rate that
the gases could be burnt by the air passing over the fire
from the firedoor. It also prevented waste due to excessive firing before or on a rising gradient. It was
better to use the coal on the grate as a reservoir of
heat to be drawn on when the engine was working hard,
than to make a large increase in the rate of firing,
bringing down the temperature in the firebox and causing
black smoke. In Controlled Firing the reservoir was
built up again on the down gradient by continuing to add
coal at the regular two-minute intervals. The number of
shovels of coal to be fired depended upon the work the
engine had to do and the fireman's guide to this was the
maintenance of his boiler pressure on the gauge.
Controlled Firing, of course, did not dispense with the
fireman's knowledge of the road, when to use the injector
and when to cease firing, but it laid down sound princ-
iples which, when combined with his road experience,
enabled him to fire an engine with efficiency and
economy.

This then was the theory. However, there were certain
difficulties in practice which require elaboration.

To be properly executed, Controlled Firing required a
high degree of skill, knowledge and confidence in
oneself, one's driver and the locomotive. There were so
many variables to be taken into account that even an
experienced fireman could get into trouble before he
realised it. Different engine classes obviously had
different characteristics and these had to be learned.
To complicate things, no individual engine in the same
class behaved in exactly the same way. Some always
steamed, or ran, better than others. Furthermore the
same engine would itself vary from month to month, week
to week or day to day, depending on that particular
period between 'shopping', its general state of repair,
whether it needed washing out, the type of coal in the
tender, etc., etc. This is what made every firing turn
such an exciting challenge.

Apart from the actual locomotive, one had just as many
variations with drivers. Some hammered engines merci-
lessly all the time, some occasionally; some never. Some
worked them so lightly that anything but the thinnest of
fires never had sufficient blast to burn brightly. Some
drove inconsistently, seemingly at a whim of the phases

of the moon, the weather, or the state of their livers,
while a row with the wife could be detected by the
position of the regulator or reversing screw. Some were
very consistent, both good and bad, and some were down-
right geniuses, but no two drivers were ever the same.
They, too, had to be learned. Then of course route
knowledge was very important. Knowing just when the
major effort was needed; where you didn't want much
steam; where you could clean the fire if necessary or
where you could drag coal forward from the back of the
tender, and when you could snatch a quick sandwich.
Controlled Firing, therefore, could not always be
strictly adhered to, since so many other factors influ-
encing the modus operandi were not controllable, but it
provided a sound guideline from which to work. Many old
drivers I found, though, tended to regard it with
suspicion.

In the early 1950s some of the unpleasant hangovers
from the war years were still very much in evidence.
Run-down equipment, poor fuel, congested lines, and a
shortage of labour in nearly every department. This
latter included firemen and experienced men were at a
premium. Although every effort was made to keep the
inexperienced on the more lowly turns, sometimes a young
Passed Cleaner found himself standing in for a top link
man on a crack job which could be embarrassing for all
concerned.

Because drivers frequently had young firemen whose
ability was an unknown quantity, they tended to play
safe and instruct the fireman to get a good fire on.
With the old Midland men this was in any case their
habitual method of firing. The steeply sloping grates
of the Classes 2, 3 and 4 goods engines responded well
to a box filled up to the firehole, and these were the
principal locomotives the old drivers fired on, the
doctrine being that it was better to have too much steam
rather than too little. Unhappily this did not always
work out. Understandably, many young firemen abandoned
their Controlled Firing theory under the pressure of
these influences and only some re-discovered its benefits in the light of their future experiences.

Eventually our period of training came to an end and
the happy day arrived, twelve weeks after joining
British Railways when, with some trepidation, we
presented ourselves to Mr.Welch for our Passing Out
test. This consisted of oral questions on the basic
workings of a locomotive, and some of the more important

rules and regulations regarding enginemen. We were taken first to a Class 3F in the shed and later to a Class 8F, and questioned on the names and functions of various parts of these engines. The examination was then conducted on the footplate where, individually, we were questioned on the controls. After this, we were required to fire a few shovels of coal; it was considered adequate if you could get two out of three shovelsful through the firehole without letting go of the shovel. The most important part of the test was taken last - to operate both injectors. This accomplished, we joined our nervous colleagues to await the verdict. Most of us passed first time and so, full of elation, we were unleashed for better or for worse on the rest of Saltley.

As Passed Cleaners, we were given a different works
number and were required to book on and off with the rest
of the enginemen. Since we were not yet matched with a
regular driver and allocated to a link roster, time of
booking on and the job involved for the following day
were obtained from the shed foreman's clerk on signing
off.

My first firing turn began at the relatively civilised
hour of 6.00 a.m., when I was assigned to the rather
uninspiring job known as loco shunt. The requirements
here were not very exacting, and were ideal for breaking
in young Passed Cleaners. The whole operation was
conducted in a quiet and leisurely way, which was just as
well since the engine used was frequently fit for nothing
else. This often took the form of the oldest Class 2F;
whilst it remained in the confines of the shed yard, all
the parts which fell off during the day could be
collected up and given to an apprentice fitter for
re-assembly during the night. At least this was the
conclusion I quickly arrived at. My mate, I found, was
in a similar condition to the engine, being in the twi-
light of his railway career. He had, therefore, lost
much of his boyish enthusiasm but I experienced the
thrill of being asked to move the engine on my very first
day.

Moving that old 2F was also a leisurely operation.
First one applied the steam brake. The control for this
was a small brass wheel mounted centrally on the boiler
face between the water gauges. It operated like a tap,
clockwise to close, anti-clockwise to open - and it took
a long time. However, a half-inch spanner was tied to
the boss with a piece of twine and by flicking the
spanner the wheel could be revolved at a fair speed.
2Fs were fitted with this unofficial modification. As
the brake valve was opened, a number of groans and clunks
from beneath the frames denoted that it had taken effect,
thus enabling the tender hand brake to be released. The
reversing lever was pushed into the full forward
position, and the brake valve closed. Loud hissings
would result, and the cab filled with steam exhausted
from the brake cylinder. This usually cleared from the
cab in about the same time as it took for the brake

blocks to release from the wheels, so that the regulator
could then be opened. The route from the regulator to
the steam chest must have been more than somewhat
complex, because for a time nothing happened. Eventually
a hiss of gradually increasing volume announced its
arrival at the other end and then after a heart-rending
sigh the old girl would judder into motion and gently
wheeze off, shrouded in its own little fog of steam.
Nothing much to raise the blood pressure of an onlooker
but great stuff to me.

The duties of the shunt were varied, but it could be
loosely described as moving anything that wanted moving.
This might involve replacing a filled wagon with an empty
one on the ashpit hopper or assembling coal wagons for
feeding the coaling plant. The latter operation frequently caused great consternation, since it entailed
actually moving off the shed limits and temporarily
blocking traffic moving into and out of the depot.
Even a dampish rail would cause loss of adhesion and I
quickly developed the technique of walking alongside the
engine sprinkling sand, clinker or ash on to the track
with the firing shovel. However, it was all very
instructive, and I soon became familiar with the various
shed roads and the points controlling them, but moving
around the loco yard was always a strenuous occupation
for a fireman as it meant haring along in front of the
engine in order to pull the points over for the required
direction, at the same time trying to keep one's feet on
oil-soaked sleepers and avoid the numerous bric-a-brac
and debris which always seemed to be lying around. As
my week on the loco shunt drew to a close I realised
that I had learned quite a lot more about shed routine,
apart from gaining experience and confidence in actually
firing and handling a locomotive, so I looked forward
more eagerly to what the following week would bring.

It happened to be another shunting turn, but this time
the real thing just across the main line from the depot
in Lawley Street marshalling yards. We booked on at
4.00 p.m. and so I enjoyed my first spell of operating an
engine at night - much the same as operating in daylight
except that you tend to rely more on touch than on sight.
It was about this time that I became finally convinced
that everything one touched on a locomotive is either
very hot, very cold, very dirty or very rough. I therefore took to wearing leather gloves, and found them so
satisfactory that I was never without a pair or two for
the remainder of my firing career. The main advantage of

protecting my hands was that I could instantly grab
anything and operate or use it without fear of acquiring
a first-degree burn. My days in the time office bore
witness to the quite serious injuries inflicted on firemen's hands during the course of their normal work.
After all, a hand flung out to save a stumble on a wildly
oscillating footplate would leave another few square
inches of skin sizzling away on the boiler front.

Shunting in Lawley Street could require some quite
strenuous work from the locomotive, not to mention the
crew, and for this we were provided with a Class 3F. I
soon discovered that these were a vast improvement in
every way over the 2Fs. They were of course somewhat
larger, but the uplift in power seemed very much greater
than the increase in size would appear to indicate,
although this may have been in part an illusion caused
by their crisp, raucous exhaust note. They were
certainly much more comfortable. The boilers were
higher pitched, giving rise to a more spacious cab which
afforded a considerably greater degree of protection
from the elements. Later, when in the Bank Pilot link,
I found that they could be made very cosy indeed with the
aid of a tarpaulin or two. Large, wooden-topped boxes
fitted either side of the cab provided very adequate
seats for both driver and fireman and, at the same time,
acted as storage lockers for the various impedimenta such
as tools, oil cans, feeders, etc., that were normally
carried. These boxes were of sufficient acreage to
double up as beds when the opportunity presented itself
to snatch forty winks. The only drawback as far as the
fireman was concerned was that the sight feed lubricator
to the cylinders was located on the side of the cab above
his head. If the drain plug was not a particularly good
fit, then a form of chinese water torture could take
place as hot emulsified oil dropped at regular intervals
into one's eyes.

With a 3F, about 70 per cent of power would be
developed on what drivers termed the first regulator. As
the regulator was pushed across the quadrant resistance
was felt when the handle was in approximately the verti-
cal position. Considerable effort - sometimes very
considerable effort - was then required to move it right
across to fully open. The final half of its travel was
called the second regulator. Most shunting operations
were generally accomplished by using the first regulator
only. For one thing, performance was satisfactory, but
the main deterrent to drivers who were relegated to

shunting duties through lack of physical fitness, or who
were anyway in their sixties, was the amount of extra
muscle power that would be required.

Reversing too was a very speedy operation with a 3F,
since they were equipped with a reversing lever and not a
screw. One mighty heave, or push, on this massive bar of
steel was all that was required. During a busy shunting
session the driver could be heaving, pushing or pulling
something almost continuously for periods of up to an
hour or so. It was little wonder that many were very
pleased on these occasions to exchange places with the
firemen who were, needless to say, only too happy to
oblige.

Shunting usually came in bursts of intense activity
followed by a period of rest. This, of course, was prog-
rammed to the arrival of incoming traffic, which seemed
to present itself in bunches of three or four trains in
quick succession. During these periods of work, quite a
fair amount of steam was required, and this proved to be
useful training in that it helped to improve my firing
technique. I also had to make some attempt at cleaning
the fire on this shift and, being my first introduction
to this common chore, did so with some difficulty. All
locomotives carried three fireirons. These consisted of
a shovel, either of the long or short variety, a rake,
which likewise could be long or short, and a dart which
might be straight or bent into a curve so that the point
could be at anything up to 90 degrees to the handle. On
a 3F it was usual to carry a short shovel, short rake and
a bent dart, this combination proving most suitable for
their relatively short, steeply sloping grates. In
Lawley Street yard the specified place for cleaning fires
was at the water column near the goods shed and this was
accomplished during a lull in the operations set aside
for the purpose of replenishing the tank. Although
considered stocky and well-muscled for my age, I was
still far from the full development of manhood and, even
though the fireirons were of the short variety, they
seemed to me to weigh about a ton each. They were
usually stowed on the back of the tender so the technique
was that, having clambered topsides and put the bag - the
leather hose attached to water columns - into the tank,
one scrambled forward over the coal, hauling the fireirons to a position easily reached from the footplate.
First, live fire was pushed away from the back corners of
the firebox using the shovel or rake, so that it formed a
sort of barrier under the brick-arch. The clinker and

ash thus exposed then had to be broken up and dislodged
from the firebars. The bent dart was the implement for
this job, being able to curl over the firehole mouthpiece
and get right into the back corners. If the clinker was
thick or hard, and it was often both, the work was really
tough. Handling those heavy fireirons soon made my arms
ache with such intensity that I thought the very sinews
had been torn. After breaking up and pushing the clinker
forward, it then had to be ladled out of the firebox and
thrown over the side of the footplate. The shovel was of
course required for this, digging it in under the clinker
using the coal barrier as a limit stop. Care had to be
taken when withdrawing the shovel back through the firehole, since any piece falling off would end up in
precisely the same place whence it originally came. I
was very appreciative of my gloves at this stage. With
iron being an excellent conductor of heat, the handle
rapidly became nearly as hot as the blade which was
continually being dipped into glowing coals. Even so, I
always supplemented the insulation provided by the gloves
with a wiper folded up to form a thick pad of cloth.
Like the ship's cook at sea, it was advisable first to
determine from which direction the wind, if any, was
blowing. If not thrown out on the lee side, a great
cloud of hot, gritty ash would quickly arrive back on
board again on to any sweaty exposed part of the crew.
Having removed all the clinker from the rear half of the
grate, live fire was then dragged back with the rake and
the area under the brick-arch attacked in a similar
manner, the only difference being that generally less
clinker formed here and it could be shovelled out without
resorting to the dart. When thoroughly clean, the
remaining live fire was spread over the grate area and
fresh coal applied to build it up to a suitable working
level.

With its relatively good fuel and water capacity, good
visibility, adequately lively performance and crew
comforts, the Class 3F seemed as well suited to shunting
as it was to the many other duties it was called upon to
perform. They belonged to a small clan of locomotives
which seemed to enjoy universal popularity amongst
enginemen. The Stanier Black Five and later, to some
extent, the B.R. Class 9 were two others that spring to
mind. I looked for a common denominator and found that
primarily all were good steamers, their boilers being
well capable of supplying all that was demanded from
them. They all rode well, were free-running, and their

cabs were roomy.

My week at Lawley Street passed quickly by. Again, I
had learned a lot and wanted to know more. I could clean
a fire, albeit somewhat slowly; I could generate enough
steam for an hour's continuous shunting; I could clean
and trim lamps and what was more important, I had
acquired a taste to see and hear a steam locomotive being
worked hard. The next fortnight brought a mixture of
jobs, booking on at every odd hour round the clock.
Every day I was acquiring fresh knowledge, seeing new
places and gaining more skill. As one old driver said to
me, 'You'll get all the glamour you want later. Let the
basic fundamentals sink in first - it takes a long time
to become really good at this job.' He was right!
Whilst a fair bit of this mixture of jobs involved shed
work, some of them did take me farther afield.

Leaving the loco yard and heading north along a sort
of chasm between the two major parts of the gas works,
one soon arrived at Saltley station, and a few hundred
yards beyond this on both sides of the main line lay that
great complex of sidings loosely known as Washwood Heath,
divided into eight separate sections: 1) the up reception (Hill 60) leading into 2) Washwood Heath up sidings
and through to Bromford, 3) Washwood Heath Junction up
sidings, 4) Washwood Heath Junction down sidings,
5) Washwood Heath down arrival lines, 6) Washwood Heath
old coal bank, 7) Washwood Heath down coal sidings, and
8) Washwood Heath goods sidings - better known as the
West End. Travelling north, the entrance to the up
reception sidings was effected from the goods line under
the shadow of the massive Washwood Heath gas holders -
well-known landmarks on the Birmingham skyline. At the
entrance, the track divided into three roads, and you did
not quite know which you would be directed along until
the points were actually visible. Permissive block
workings were operated here, which meant that contact
with the brake van of the proceeding train could be made
at any place, so extreme caution was necessary. These
three roads were laid over what amounted to an elongated
hump, halfway along which a gantry spanned the tracks
carrying three stop signals, and under these three
calling-on signals. The hump dipped sharply at the far
end, leading into the numerous sidings which ran right
through to Bromford, the outlet for the north. The hump
was colloquially known as Hill 60, after its notorious
counterpart on the Western Front in World War I.

My first contact with Hill 60 caused me some alarm.

We had relieved a mixed freight from Worcester at Landor
Street Junction (almost opposite the shed), which was
hauled by a Class 3F. Having rolled gently down the up
goods line through the aforesaid chasm, past Saltley
station, we were diverted on to Hill 60. I had not
travelled so far before, so I was skipping from one side
of the footplate to the other, all agog to see what new
vistas of scenic wonder lay in store for me around each
curve of the track. I was considerably surprised, therefore, to see all three roads blocked by trains and,
finding that we were on the centre one, quickly
calculated that we would be into the rear of that
particular train in about twenty seconds. With rising
panic, I rapidly drew my driver's attention to the fact
for, although travelling at little more than a good
walking pace, I had visions of soon being picked out of a
heap of matchwood. His retort was a calm 'O.K., mate,
I've seen it.' A few seconds later he closed the regulator and with barely a touch of the brakes, we eased
gently up against the brake van. I breathed a sigh of
relief and sat down. This action provoked a frown from
my driver, and his subsequent words contained a trace of
annoyance. 'Carry on, then,' says he. 'Carry on what?'
says I, frantically doing a mental scan of my training
notes to think of something important I might have
missed. His voice broke in on my thoughts. 'Don't you
know what to do? Never mind, son,' he said with gentle
tolerance, 'I'll explain all about it. Just couple the
brake van to our engine, take the headlamp off the smokebox top bracket and put it on the tender, and then come
back here.' I did as instructed and returned to the
footplate, where my mate filled me in on this procedure.

There were three arrival roads, and if empty, trains
were hauled through to the far end and halted at the
shunter's cabin just before the tracks dipped sharply
into the sidings. The locomotive was then uncoupled and
set off to the shed or other duties as required. To save
having an engine solely for the purpose of shunting this
train, it remained on the arrival road until another
train turned up behind it. The shunter then checked the
destination labels, chalked a siding number on the front
of the wagons and uncoupled them as appropriate. When
he was ready the calling-on signal was pulled off and the
engine, having been attached as previously described,
slowly pushed the original train over the hump, at the
same time pulling its own train into position. The
wagons trickled slowly at first, then with ever

increasing momentum into the dip, where a small horde of
junior shunters and brakesmen leapt frantically hither
and thither pulling points and dropping brakes, endeav-
ouring to ensure that the right wagon entered the right
siding at the right speed.

Sometimes the wagons moved over the top singly, when
their motion could be easily checked, sometimes in twos
or threes and sometimes in great rafts of twenty or more!
These fairly hurtled down into the sidings and not even
the most agile brakesman could do more than make a token
gesture of dropping perhaps a single brake handle. So
great was their momentum that they could run right
through to the Bromford end if the road was empty. In
later years I was to witness a number of these spectacular and dangerous instances. More usually, though, they
would finally come to rest against a train of wagons
already standing on that particular road, when they would
dissipate their energy in a most tremendous crash. At
night these crashes and bangs could be heard for miles
around - most irritating if you were standing in a nearby
siding trying to get a spot of shut-eye. Needless to
say, this method of shunting, while economical in motive
power, was very heavy on the wagons and disastrous for
their contents. Wagons and vans could be seen with their
end planking burst asunder by the violence of the impacts
as their loads were transferred in the form of missiles
to the next wagon in the train. A multitude of comp-
laints arose from this form of vandalism but the method
persisted.

Now I knew all about the up sidings at Washwood Heath,
that is except for one thing. 'Why did you get me to put
the headlamp on the tender while we were still attached
to the train?' I asked as we arrived at the shunter's
cabin. My driver smiled a benevolent smile. 'Merely to
save your legs, my lad. You would only have had to do it
now. As it is, we're all ready to go off to the shed.'
Economy of effort was always the byword of experienced
enginemen.

Later that week I worked a local trip job as far as
Water Orton, some seven miles from Saltley and the
farthest north of what can be considered the Birmingham
area sidings network. This was the departure point of
Saltley's premier jobs - the Carlisles! The crews for
these crack long-distance express freights were treated
with the reverence of royalty, and I watched with a mixed
feeling of awe and envy as these beautifully-turned-out
Black Fives blasted their way into the distance on their

226-mile run north. I never realised then that some
eight years later I too would be receiving the red
carpet treatment as one of the elite crews privileged to
work the Carlisles and Glasgows. Nor did I realise that
this would entail the hardest continuous physical effort
I'd ever have to endure.

With some disappointment I found I was booked to work
the whole of the following week shunting at Water Orton
and, to make matters worse, I had to work with not a
Saltley driver but one of three permanently stationed at
Water Orton solely for this duty. Little did I know that
this was to prove just about the happiest week I ever
spent as a Passed Cleaner. Water Orton sidings could be
divided into four parts. The centre, with a capacity of
173 wagons, dealt mainly with traffic to and from
Walsall, Wolverhampton and points beyond. The marshalling sidings, capable of holding 918 wagons, had a long
shunting spur at the west end. Here freight, both local
and from the south and west, was sorted and assembled to
form the northbound trains. The stowing sidings were
unique in having flat rails (rails laid on their sides)
and as the name implies were used only for this purpose.
On the other side of the main line was a small siding
known as 'Under the Wood'. Part belonged to the
engineers' department, the rest being used to detach
traffic destined for Walsall, from through freight
trains travelling south. The shunt was required to do
all the sorting out which this busy marshalling yard
demanded, and was therefore frequently called upon to
perform a fair amount of very hard work.

In 1950, diesels had not infiltrated into all the
shunting turns and, although one would have suited the
exacting requirements of this shunt admirably (single
manning, long duration and 24-hour availability), none
had then been allocated. A ubiquitous Class 3F therefore performed the function in its usual lively and
raucous manner, being allowed a couple of hours off
around mid-week to go back to the shed for stores and
coal. I was told to book on at 12.40 p.m. so that I
could walk down to Saltley station and catch the
1.05 p.m. slow to Water Orton. For the first time
since 'passing out', I felt lonely and somewhat worried
as to how this week would work out. Also I had not
been told by what means I was to return home after
relief. However, I need not have concerned myself over
this latter point. The system was simple. The signalman merely stopped a suitable passing freight long

enough for me to hop on board and I then rode with it to
within reasonable walking distance from the shed. With
the goods line blocked with traffic, though, this reasonable walking distance could mean a fifty-minute hike
along the track from Bromford.

I duly arrived at Water Orton station and, after a few
false starts, eventually located my engine which was
standing rather forlornly near to the shunter's cabin.
She was 3284, equipped with a 3,250-gallon Johnson tender
without coal bulkhead. On these tenders a small
partition about 3' high, on which the tool box was
mounted, served to retain the coal. The number on the
cab side was just discernible through the usual layer of
dirt which unfortunately most engines seemed to be
ingrained with in those days. There was no sign of
anyone about, so I clambered aboard, stowed my kit in
the tender locker and did a quick check of boiler and
fire. The water level was just out of sight in the top
of the gauge glass and the fire, nicely thin under the
arch, had a good body in the back corners and also looked
relatively clean. The tender was well filled with coal
of surprisingly good quality - so good in fact that I
couldn't help feeling that someone had sneaked under the
passenger end of the coaling hopper. I was, moreover,
pleased to see that the footplate had been brushed and
hosed down, indicating that the previous crew still had a
pride in their job.

Feeling something like a member of the boarding party
who discovered the 'Marie Celeste', I thought it would be
prudent to see if I could find the missing crew. In
later years experience taught me to look first in the
nearest cabin, but on this particular occasion it took a
few minutes before the logical deduction was arrived at.
Once the penny had dropped, I trundled up to the cabin,
knocked politely on the door and after a suitable pause,
entered. I was greeted by looks of what can only be
described as a mixture of blank amazement, anxiety and
incredulity. It was, of course, usual for firemen to
burst in unannounced. This knocking obviously had them
rattled, thinking no doubt that they had been paid a
surprise visit by the chief of the operating department.
Mild annoyance quickly replaced their former expressions.
'Don't bloody well knock if you ever come here again,'
growled a burly character who turned out to be Sam, the
head shunter. I apologised profusely and announced who I
was. A lean, friendly chap in his mid-thirties wearing
enginemen's overalls immediately leaped up, made the

brief statement that everything was okay, that in fact
the old girl was quite a good 'un, that his mate was in
the local with a pint already waiting for him, and that
Joe (my driver) would no doubt be along in due course.
He then departed hastily, heading in the general direction of the Dog & Duck, leaving me in sole charge. During
my railway career I was to see many instances where, in
order to expedite the job, rules - if not actually broken
- were certainly severely bent. Only on the odd
occasions when the various trade unions thought it
necessary to adhere strictly to the rules did operations
come virtually to a standstill.

I eased out of the cabin with as much dignity as I
could muster in the circumstances, and proceeded to
conduct what I thought would be interpreted as a
business-like inspection of our engine. Absorbed in
this, I suddenly became aware that a rather high-pitched
squeaky voice was addressing me. 'Are you my mate?' I
answered that if he was Joe, then I was indeed his mate.
'Is she all right?' said Joe affably enough. 'I think
so,' I replied. 'At any rate, the other fireman said she
was.' 'Well, if Alan said so, that's good enough for
me,' he squeaked. Joe was of very slight build which
could only be described as generally bent. That is to
say, his shoulders were hunched and his legs bowed, the
combined effect of which reduced his height to about
5' 3". His face bore the marks of long exposure to the
elements and could be likened to that of a walnut, for he
looked much older than his actual 64 years. His demeanour was mild, gentle and considerate and I couldn't help
taking to him at once. This old chap, I thought, needs
all the assistance I can give him.

The first bit of help was not long in coming. 'We had
better get aboard,' said Joe. He grasped the hand rails,
laboriously hauled himself up to the second step and
promptly stuck fast. 'Give me a bunk-up, mate. The
rheumatism has got my knees again,' he panted. I applied
a shoulder to his rear end and projected him onto the
footplate, wondering at the same time how he was going to
cope with a hectic bout of shunting. Once on board, I
opened the damper, turned on the blower and shot half a
dozen shovels of coal down the front end of the firebox,
where the bars were now showing. Joe pulled out an
ancient pocket watch and the myopic manner in which he
studied this should have given me a clue as to the next
brick-bat he was about to drop. 'We shall start shunting
in ten minutes, so I wonder if you would mind clearing as

much coal as you can from my side of the tender over to
yours. I can't lean out so easily with this rheumatism,
and my eyes aren't what they were, so it helps if I can
see over the top of the tender.' This was, of course, a
very sound practice which I often came across on the bank
pilots and trip workings involving a fair amount of
tender-first running. Vastly improved vision could be
achieved by levelling the coal on the driver's side, and
this was particularly effective on the low-built Johnson
tenders. I had nearly completed this task when Sam,
equipped with shunting pole, leaped on the bottom engine
steps, thrust his head between the hand rails, and yelled
in a powerful baritone, 'Right, Joe, let's get cracking.'
We eased slowly back on to a long line of mixed vans and
wagons, leaving a trail of steam spluttering from the
open cylinder drain cocks. Sam coupled up at the instant
the buffers touched, and scampered off down the train to
check that all was well. In the meantime I took the
opportunity to build up a good body of fire, since I
wanted to see just how things were done in this particular yard. I soon discovered that practically all the
shunting was accomplished from the driver's side, thereby
relieving the fireman of that somewhat onerous duty of
verbally translating the shunter's hand signals. This
would have required constant vigilance achievable only by
leaning half out of the cab and bellowing at the top of
your voice such choice phrases as, 'Hitemup!' or
'Whoa-up!'

Apart from ensuring that we had a good fire and
keeping the boiler reasonably full, and with a Class 3F
neither of these requirements posed much difficulty, I
thought that I was going to have a relatively easy time.
However, it wasn't long before it became apparent that
Joe was having difficulty in sighting Sam's signals. He
called me over to his side of the footplate. 'Can you
make out what Sam wants? I can't see him very well when
he stands against a dark background,' said Joe, desperately wiping the moisture from his eyes. I peeped over
the side, and was surprised to see Sam only some 150
yards away making frantic circular motions with his arm,
indicating that he wished us to draw forward. Admittedly
he was against a dark background but he had a large piece
of newspaper in his hand and I could clearly see that the
expression on Sam's face was one of extreme exasperation.
Joe's eyesight was worse than I thought and so for the
next hour and a half I remained in station on that side
of the footplate acting as his eyes and ears. I say ears

as well, because Sam reinforced his hand signals with a
bellow that could be clearly heard half a mile away. As
we slammed the successive rakes of wagons backwards and
forwards, I noticed that Joe's efforts became slower and
more laboured. The old chap was visibly distressed; he
could manage the regulator, which was quite free-moving
on the first valve, without too much trouble, but the
continual need to heave the heavy reversing lever to and
fro was taking its toll. Seeing him suffering thus, I
was debating whether he would think it presumptuous of me
to offer to take over when, during a brief lull in the
operations, he suddenly gasped, 'Well, you've seen how
it's done, mate. Would you like to have a go this side
now?' This was exactly what I had been itching to do for
the past hour! Joe flopped on the fireman's seat,
reaching for the tea can, and with as much control as I
could muster I took up position on the driver's platform.

Sam was ready for us to draw ahead again, with a new
train to be shunted. I would show 'em, I thought,
flinging the reversing lever into forward gear with great
gusto and pushing the regulator open in an equally
sprightly manner. We puffed off in a lively fashion for
a few yards when a terrific lurch sent me staggering and
Joe's tea everywhere except the place he wanted it.
'Ease it open gently to start with, until you take up the
slack in the couplings and feel the weight of the train,'
Joe advised tolerantly. 'Then you can give it some
stick.' This was the first of many points I was soon to
learn. We chugged forward gaining speed while I stared
intently at Sam. Suddenly he flung up both arms. As
quick as a flash I slammed shut the regulator and pushed
the brake handle right across. Bang, bang, bang! A
series of powerful buffets shot a couple of hundredweight
of coal on to the footplate and more tea over Joe's
overalls. Moreover, we ran well past the spot where Sam
had wanted us to stop. I glanced anxiously at Joe.
'It's the same thing when you want to stop,' he said.
'Only the other way round. Give it a bit of brake to
close up the couplings first and then when you feel the
push of the train, give it the lot.' It had all looked
so easy when Joe was driving, but then an expert makes
the most difficult things seem like child's play. I had
a lot to learn yet and the next lesson was soon forth-
coming.

Sam's stentorian voice rent the air. 'Hitemup!' He
was calling me back in his usual vigorous style. This
time I eased the regulator open until I felt the wagons

buffer up and then I gave it full first valve. We surged
back in a grand spurt of acceleration. Sam deftly
detached the couplings a few wagons from the end and then
raised both arms into the air. I snatched the regulator
shut and applied the brake almost in one movement - very
slick, I thought. A violent pull again sent me reeling,
whilst a loud crack and a cloud of brown dust drifted
across the scene. To my horror I saw that we only had
two wagons attached to the engine and the thirty or so
which should have been there were trundling obediently
after the six that Sam had detached. I had committed the
cardinal sin of breaking the train. Too late I realised
that, as before, I should first have given a gentle check
to stretch out the couplings and then on feeling the pull
of the train, rendered the final full application. Joe
pointed this out, while Sam's only comment was, 'Just
make sure that you don't break more than one shackle per
wagon, otherwise I'll have nothing to hook on with.'
Having digested these basic shunting rules, I was gradually able to work faster and more effectively, and by
the end of the shift both Joe and Sam seemed satisfied
with my efforts. I did not break any more couplings and
we were not getting thrown around the footplate. I was,
therefore, feeling quite pleased with myself when I
hitched a lift back to Saltley in the brake van of a
passing Class B freight. This was my first ride of any
distance in the brake of a loose-coupled train; it was
to prove very interesting and undoubtedly affected my
approach to driving in the future.

    The train was still stationary as I stumbled up the
steps on to the rear verandah of the van. It was now
quite dark and it took a little time before I managed to
locate the position of the door and operate its unfamiliar handle. I groped my way inside the pitch black
cavern, where nothing was to be seen but a small red
glow indicating the position of the stove. 'Anyone at
home?' I called. 'I'm the fireman off the shunt. Do
you mind if I cadge a lift to the West End?' 'Not at
all,' came the answer. 'Although you'll probably wish
that you had picked someone else. It's Piggy Trayner
driving.' Here the voice paused, and I sensed that this
name should have conveyed some significance to me but,
as it did not, I merely replied 'Oh.' 'You had better
show the "bobby" a light,' said the voice, which turned
out to belong to one Bill Bodkin, a goods guard of some
seniority. 'Here, take my lamp, but hang on tight when
we go.' So saying, Bill pulled a hand lamp from where

it had been wedged in a corner of the van and passed it
to me. I leaned over the side and waved it in the
general direction of the signal box. The signalman must
have been looking out for this because almost instantly
our signal was pulled off. I headed for the interior
again and had just made the portal when the clank of
tautening couplings could be heard rapidly approaching.
I grasped the door frame, bearing in mind what Bill had
advised, and the next moment found myself flying through
the air to fetch up with an almighty crash which knocked
every bit of breath out of my body, against the brake
boards of the brake van. We had instantly accelerated
from a dead stand to 10m.p.h. in about two yards! As I
struggled to regain my feet, a violent bang shot me
forwards this time, against the ashpan of the stove.
Next came a series of minor tremors lasting about a
minute and then quiet serenity reigned, broken only by
the click, click of wheels over rail joints.

'Good grief,' I gasped. 'What happened?' 'That,'
hissed Bill through clenched teeth, 'is Sam's usual way
of showing disapproval of being held up. Mind you, he's
no more gentle at the best of times, so sit down and
wedge yourself in like this.' He again adopted a knees
up, arms braced configuration. I did likewise.

That journey back to Washwood Heath was a real eye-
opener, and showed me at firsthand just what sort of
treatment a thoughtless or unsympathetic driver could
mete out to anyone travelling at the rear end of a
loose-coupled train. Every check was accompanied by a
series of buffets and surges, even slight changes in
gradient giving a similar effect, whilst the starts were
positively nerve-racking. One could not relax for a
second and I was very pleased indeed to escape from this
torture chamber after only a few miles. How Bill and
his colleagues stood it for fifty or more miles I will
never know. 'Haven't you told him about it?' I asked
Bill after a particularly powerful clout finally
announced our arrival at the West End. 'Many times,'
said Bill wearily. As I cycled home that night I vowed
that if ever I came to drive trains I would concentrate
on that very aspect of the technique. I did not know
then that in time I would have a very much more intimate
relationship with Sam 'Piggy' Trayner.

The following day I just could not get back to work
at Water Orton soon enough. I had thoroughly digested
the previous day's experiences, going over my mistakes
again and again until I had at least mentally eradicated

them. Joe had also intimated that for the rest of the
week he would be quite happy to let me do the driving.
After a bout of hectic shovelling when I arrived and a
quick check around, I announced that I was ready to
commence. 'Right, back up then,' called Sam, yanking
over a couple of point levers. Steam brake on, wind the
hand brake off, small ejector open, lever into back gear,
steam brake off, regulator open! We chuffed backwards,
leaving the cylinder drain cocks (known as the taps to
enginemen) open so as to clear any residual condensation
from the cylinders. Without Joe on the footplate I felt
remarkably at ease. Yesterday's training had certainly
given me confidence and I was at that moment sublimely
happy. It all seemed so natural that I might have been
doing it for years and, although I admittedly needed the
polish which can only be acquired through long practice,
I had at least grasped the basic essentials. Clunk!
With a deft wristy movement Sam hooked on. 'We've got a
big one first,' he yelled. 'So you'll have to draw well
forward - off you go then!' I pushed the reversing
lever into full forward gear, closed the taps, and eased
open the regulator. Leaning well out, I could see each
wagon gently rock into motion as the couplings tautened.
I was also now sensitive enough to feel successive little
checks as the weight of every individual wagon added its
bulk to the strain, and I had to inch the regulator
farther open to counteract this steadily increasing load.
A faint wiggle from the last wagon was sufficient indication for me to pounce on the regulator and to thrust it
on to full first valve. As that beautifully crisp blast
rent the warm, still air, I was surprised to find how far
I had already opened the regulator getting the train
underway. This was a heavy one indeed and called for
sterner stuff than just full first valve. So far I had
not worked the engine beyond this position. There had
really been no need but now, with something of an excuse,
I pushed it right across! Very little difference could
be detected initially, and I kept my hands on the
regulator handle poised to slam it shut should she slip,
but the old girl was very sure-footed and the rail was
dry. Suddenly she seemed to get the bit between her
teeth, the blast sharpened and it became obvious that we
were accelerating this great load very vigorously indeed.
I quickly kicked the firehole doors shut with the idea
that this powerful blast would liven the fire up somewhat. It certainly did, for a towering column of black
smoke rocketed skywards. Doubtless Mr.Welch would have

had something to say about that, but what the hell - if
we sounded impressive, then we might as well look impressive too. . . .

No other form of locomotion is as demonstratively
powerful as a steam engine at full chat and I was so
enthralled at this spectacle that I almost forgot Sam.
Looking back along the train I was just in time to see
him throw up his arms. So, regulator shut, a touch of
brake to close up the train, then full brake. An
almighty surge as the weight came into us but none of the
crashing and banging of yesterday's shock tactics. Too
late, I realised that if you used second regulator then
you needed to shut off just that much sooner to stop at
the required spot. Sam detached and called me back. If
this 'right across' method gave more power to our elbow
then I might as well use it as often as possible, I
thought. Over went the regulator and we charged back in
a veritable welter of sparks, smoke and noise. This
time I anticipated Sam by a few wagon lengths and already
had the brake on by the time he signalled me to stop.
This was the secret then - anticipation! As we pelted
into rake after rake of wagons, I gradually developed the
technique, so that I was able to halt in just about the
right place for Sam every time, and the minutes this
saved added up to a sizable amount by the end of the
shift. I must admit that I was more than ready for a
break when, after a couple of hours, Sam stopped me
outside the cabin. Our mutual enthusiasm was undoubtedly infectious for everyone had worked like blazes.
Full regulator work had called for more firing than
usual, and every brief pause found me with the shovel in
my hands, apart from frequent use of the injector.

'Come and get a cup of tea,' called Sam. 'I reckon
we've earned it.' As I clambered down from the
footplate, he addressed me in a quiet tone. 'Do you
know, that's the fastest piece of shunting I've done in
many a long day. These old fellows won't let 'em rip
like that. Well done, kid!' This compliment from a man
who normally did not go out of his way to say much
pleased me no end, and made me more than ever determined
to work at maximum effort when conditions would allow.

After the welcome tea, Joe took up station on the
fireman's side. 'We've got to run down to the north end
to pick up wagons now, but take it easy - the track's in
a rare old state down there. Bill Wilson had her off the
road all wheels last week!' This procedure of running
down to the north end was usually necessary at least

twice a shift and was accomplished by using the empty
outside siding - for me, a completely new experience.
To say that the track was in a rare old state was an
understatement. The ballast had long since disappeared
from under the sleepers! No two sections of rail were
in the same plane, and with broken chairs and missing
keys thrown in for good measure, the general condition
was alarming. Fortunately travelling tender-first this
was not too apparent. With an open stretch of track in
front of me I gave way to a sudden impulse and notched
her up to one out of mid-gear and opened up the regulator. With a 3F, two types of gear quadrants were to be
found. In one, an evenly spaced number of notches gave
a progressive shortening of cut-off as the lever was
moved towards mid-gear. The second and more common type
had only three notches corresponding to approximately
50 per cent, 35 per cent and 20 per cent. Shortening
the cut-off was easy enough when the regulator was only
slightly open, but when on full first valve or more, and
pressure was high in the steam chest, then even
Hercules would have been a bit pushed to haul it into
the desired position. 3284 had the latter type and Joe,
looking out of the fireman's side, did not notice my
action, nor did he hear the clatter of valve gear which
accompanies the notching up act until steam pressure in
the chest builds up again. Therefore, with just a
sizzle of steam from the chimney we started to fairly
gallop along, heaving and pitching uncomfortably. Joe
stood this treatment until, with no more than half the
complement of wheels in contact with the track at any
one time, he turned towards me. 'Slow down, slow down,'
he shouted, clinging desperately to the hand rail with
one hand and the injector steam valve with the other.
Even Sam, a confirmed speed enthusiast, was on the point
of baling out from his position on the tender steps.
Joe thoroughly ticked me off for this display of exuberance and when we arrived at the north end took me down
from the footplate to inspect the track. I immediately
conceded that he had certainly good cause for anxiety,
and our future travels along siding Number Eighteen were
at much more moderate speeds.
      As the week progressed, so did my dexterity in
handling an engine. I was able to achieve a delicacy
of control with a loose-coupled train which stood me in
good stead for my future driving activities, and which
caused a certain amount of controversy with a particular
driver I was to be booked with some years in the future.

Meanwhile, Joe seemed to spend more and more time in the
cabin, only coming out to act as a deterrent to my
record-breaking inclinations along siding Number Eighteen. This pleased us all, since apart from giving the
old fellow a much easier time, I felt unfettered and
more free to expand my boisterous technique. We were
all slightly sad when I bade farewell for the last time
at the end of the week. I had made many new friends,
spent more hours at the regulator than I could ever have
dreamed possible at this early stage in my career, and
had developed a much better appreciation of the complicated chain of events which starts with a shovel of coal
and ends when the last vehicle of a train jerks into
motion.

After that glorious week at Water Orton, I was next
required to book on at 6.00 a.m. as a spare fireman. It
was fairly common practice to ensure that a number of
spare men were available at this time of the morning to
cover such contingencies as over-sleeping, sickness,
specials and extra relief work. The more important jobs
were of course allocated to the more senior firemen so
that junior Passed Cleaners like myself were left with
the dregs. On the Thursday, I was delighted to discover
that the regular fireman of the Nuneaton pick-up had not
arrived and I had to take his place. I was briefly
introduced to my driver, a round, wobbly chap whose
girth exceeded his height by quite a few inches and who,
contrary to popular belief, was not at all a happy bundle
of fun. Jack (for this was his name) disliked junior
firemen in general and Passed Cleaners in particular.
This arose from the fact that as a fireman he had not
been one of Saltley's brightest stars and, coupled with
a pathological dislike for physical work, felt that
should the fireman prove inadequate he would be unable
or unwilling to put matters right. 'How long have you
been out?' he demanded impolitely. 'Five weeks and four
days,' I answered proudly. 'Good God,' he exclaimed,
turning to the foreman's assistant. 'I'm not taking
him, he's only a bloody kid.' This left me absolutely
stunned and not a little hurt. An argument flared up,
ending only when the foreman's assistant told him that
if he didn't take me then the job would have to be
cancelled and the only alternative was shed duties.
Jack grasped me firmly by the arm and hauled me through
the lobby doorway to the engine board. 'That's our
engine, 3435, and it's over there,' he said, indicating
a 3F just discernible in the gloom on the other side of

the shed. 'Do you know how to prepare her?' 'Yes, I
think so,' I replied, feeling about half the size I had
a few minutes earlier. Jack clicked his tongue
impatiently. 'Make sure the sandboxes are full. We'll
need them up the bank, and get me a good seat.' The
seat he referred to would be a plank or board of suitable size to serve as a substitute for the original
locker lid. It was an unsolved mystery as to where
these seats went, but they invariably disappeared almost
as soon as an engine arrived from shops. This 'disease'
afflicted only Class 3F and 4F 0-6-0s and Class 2P, 3P
and 4P 4-4-0s, all others being apparently immune.
Rumour had it that steam raisers used them for fire-
lighting activities, but my own theory was that one of
the shed staff manufactured rabbit hutches or the like
as a sideline.

As we approached our engine, we met a Passed Cleaner
friend of mine carrying a bucket of tools to the stores.
This was a stroke of luck, since at that time of a
morning tools were normally scarce. They had just
disposed of an engine and had stabled it close to ours,
so I quickly relieved him of the bucket and shovel and
dashed over to strip it of the equipment I required;
two headlamps, a gauge glass lamp, coal pick and the
all-important seats. Our engine was in a filthy state,
with great clouds of 'green' smoke rolling lazily out of
both chimney and cab. Holding my breath, I clambered on
to the footplate, knocked the blower on and when the
smoke had cleared somewhat took stock of the situation.
Black smuts covered everything of course, and I had to
wipe both the pressure gauge and water gauge glasses
before I could discern that we had 50lbs. per sq.in. on
the former and that the water was out of sight in the
top nut of the latter. I opened the firehole doors
which were of the old Midland pattern, i.e., a plate
covering three-quarters of the firehole area, hinged at
the bottom and secured when in position by a latch and
chain. The upper quarter was closed by an adjustable
flap hinged from the top. I was relieved to see that
quite a reasonable deflector plate was in position and
the brick arch looked sound. A great solid mound of
mainly unburned coal was heaped in the back corners of
the firebox so I decided that I had better spread this
around first in view of the low steam pressure. I therefore required the rake which was residing, together with
a dart and clinker shovel, in their usual place on the
back of the tender. As I scrambled over the coal, I

noticed in the dim light that it consisted almost
entirely of ovoids, bricquettes and slack. It was not
the type of fuel which exactly boosts confidence, but I
was now aware of the steaming properties of 3Fs and was
therefore not too dismayed. Whilst on top of the tender,
I ran through the normal drill of making sure that everything was secure and no lumps of coal were likely to fall
off and injure any innocent bystander who might happen to
be around as we moved off the shed. With rake in hand,
I descended to the footplate and started spreading the
fire over the whole area of the grate. In later years I
never moved off the shed without checking to see if there
was any clinker in the back of the firebox, since on many
occasions I've had to do a quick cleaning job before
departing. Very often the first indication that you had
set out on a journey with a dirty fire was when the
driver started to demand steam in quantity and then it
was too late to do much about it.

With the bottom flap of the firedoor closed, I left
the fire to burn up and, armed with a seven-eighths
spanner, climbed round the cab on to the framing. From
here, I was able to lift off the sandbox covers to check
their contents before tightening the lugs on the smokebox door. After disposal it was common practice to
leave only two lugs fastened, the remainder being the
responsibility of the preparation crew. However, it was
amazing the number of occasions that engines left the
shed with insecure smokebox doors and this oversight,
needless to say, did not exactly enhance steaming
properties. Fortunately the sandboxes only needed one
bucketful each to top them up. At Saltley, dried sand
was to be found in ovens located in Number Two shed so,
depending on where your engine was stabled, a walk of
only a few yards or as much as fifty was required to
obtain sand. This was one of the most onerous tasks
involved in preparation, since the sand was carried in
what were termed buckets - similar in appearance to wide
necked watering cans and when full weighing about 60lbs.
each. Half a dozen trips with a bucket in each hand
resulted in a definite speeding up of the circulation,
and arms feeling about three inches longer than when you
started the exercise. The unwritten rule was that these
buckets should be left on one end of the turntable where
they could be seen by all, but human nature being what it
is meant that not everyone complied, and much time was
lost hunting around for them in the semi-darkness.

A series of grunts and much laboured breathing from

under the engine indicated that Jack was trying to prise
his oversized midriff into that inadequate space between
firebox and big ends in order to attempt the oiling of
the latter. Meanwhile I decided to do a spot of oiling
on my own account, and turned my attention to the sight
feed lubricator which served the cylinders. Jack had
already left the bottle of thick black oil warming on
the drip tray over the firedoor, so I only had to open
the lower drain cock to run off the residual water and
top up with oil through the filler plug. This was one
of the first things my driver had shown me on the Lawley
Street shunt since, as he quite rightly pointed out,
extra friction at the front end meant extra coal on the
fire. It was, therefore, very much in the fireman's own
interest to see that this little friend was kept filled
and working properly.

The needle was beginning to move on the pressure
gauge as the fire brightened under the influence of the
blower and I now bent to the task of clearing up the
layer of ovoids and slack that lay strewn over the footplate. There was still insufficient pressure to test
the injectors properly, so I took the opportunity to
sweep off the residual smokebox char from the framing.
Quite early on in my career I developed a distinct
dislike of having an eyeful of char every time I
happened to look round the side of the cab, so I became
very fastidious over this matter, even to the point of
checking whenever possible engines I relieved on the
road. Also, from the company's view, this practice was
to be commended since this effective abrasive blowing
into the motion did it a power of no good.

I had travelled down the starboard side of the
framing, round the smokebox, and was heading for home
along the port side when I came up against Jack's generous posterior protruding from under the boiler. It
was quite obvious that his general topography was all
wrong for this sort of work. He withdrew and, through
the grease and sweat that smeared his face, I perceived
that he regarded me now with a somewhat milder eye.
'You're a bit slimmer than me, kid,' he panted. 'See if
you can oil the inner slide bar cups.' I obliged with
alacrity, only too pleased to show him that I was not
quite as useless as he thought. Perhaps I'd given him
a quizzical look prior to squeezing under the boiler,
because he added by way of an explanation, 'My mate
usually does the oiling.' That remark did not surprise
me in the least, and I thought that this was probably

another good reason why he didn't like strange firemen. 'If you are ready, I'll get the table,' he said in a tone that lacked the former aggression. 'Well, I haven't tested the injectors yet!' I answered. 'Never mind about those,' he shouted, walking over to the table. 'There's too much water in the boiler as it is. We can do that out in the yard.'

Having filled the last cup, I slithered to the floor and joined Jack on the table as he released the second of the two locking catches. 'These apologies for steam raisers, fill 'em up to the whistle, and then we have the responsibility of trying to stop 'em when they're priming,' he grumbled irritably. Jack was of course referring to the condition of priming, the phenomenon when water is carried over into the cylinders via the regulator and main steam pipe. Apart from the possibility of knocking the ends out of the cylinders, since water is uncompressible, the alarming spectacle of an engine charging away after the regulator had been closed usually resulted. Coupled with a cold brake and lowish steam pressure, even quite experienced drivers have effected a number of speedy demolition jobs on shed walls over the years.

With the table in position, Jack returned to the engine while I stood well clear at the end of the pit. Streams of water and steam spluttered from the taps as Jack eased open the regulator. Wumph! A muffled beat indicated just what was in the cylinders and then a veritable torrent of dirty water mushroomed out of the chimney, collected the surface layer of soot from the shed roof and then descended on the immediate neighbourhood. I instinctively looked down as the deluge swept over me, and 3435 shuddered forward onto the table to stop just about on the point of balance. On the tables in Numbers One and Two sheds, it was important to position a locomotive so that the weight was evenly distributed over the centre pivot, otherwise hand cranking could be very strenuous indeed. Number Three shed's table, being more modern, was not so critical in this respect. Since we had to turn our engine through nearly 180 degrees so that it was pointing to the north, I coupled up the engine vacuum pipe to the table tractor motor, hoping that we could create sufficient inches of mercury for it to function adequately. 'Blow up,' I yelled at the top of my voice, and Jack tugged open the large ejector. More dirty water headed skyward, but when I pulled the control lever the motor settled to its

distinctive chug, chug, chug and whine of straight-cut
gears which always reminded me of a Number 36 tram car.
   With the turning operation completed, I placed the
headlamps in the light engine position, walked through
the shed entrance, set the points for the departure
road, and called Jack out. He did this cautiously,
since the boiler was still very full; meanwhile I
trotted ahead, setting the points in the yard and keeping a good lookout for other engine movements. We
needed to fill the tank, so I stationed myself at the
water column on one of the departure roads. Jack rolled
gently up and stopped at exactly the right spot. When
first passed out, I wondered how drivers always managed
to be so accurate when halting engines at water columns
without apparently looking back at the tender. This
became abundantly clear when it was explained to me that
at every column a marker, such as a lamp standard or the
like, was selected. Some part of the locomotive cab was
lined up with this marker, and then it was only a case
of remembering which part of each particular class of
engine lined up with the marker. It sounds simple, but
when you think of all the different types of engines
then in service, plus all the columns one might visit,
the number of permutations is quite staggering. No
wonder enginemen never stopped learning.
   Hopping on top of the tender, I pulled the column arm
round by means of the chain provided and wrestled the
stiff leather hose into the tank filler hole. 'O.K.,
Jack,' I shouted, when satisfied that it was in position
without any kinks. I had previously experienced having
an unintentional shower, if shower is the right word
when one receives thirty gallons of cold water travelling at high velocity square in the chest, because a bag
had been hastily and incorrectly inserted. 'If you are
all right,' called Jack when the water was running well,
'I'll go and mash the tea and ring out.' I nodded my
assent, being now capable of turning off the water and
removing the bag from the tank. With him out of the way
I could test the injectors and complete my cleaning down
operations on the footplate. In addition to removing
smokebox char from the framing I had also acquired a
taste for having a clean and tidy cab, a task which was
admittedly motivated in part by pride, but it developed
into almost an obsession in later years and I became
well known for this idiosyncrasy. Nearly all engines
were provided with a slaking pipe. This was a flexible
hose coupled via a valve to the fireman's injector and,

depending on the setting of that injector, was capable of
delivering either cool water at moderate pressure or an
extremely powerful jet of scalding hot water and steam.
This device was most suitable for disposing of every bit
of dirt and dust from the footplate and quickly brought
the footboards up to a very presentable scrubbed appearance. With the tank filled and the housework completed
I awaited Jack's return. It was most important for us to
ring out at our prescribed time. If we did not, then any
subsequent delays would be booked to the motive power
department. Providing the controller at Duddeston Road
signal box was advised that we were ready to depart on
time, any delay occurring after this would be booked to
traffic and this would not be our fault.

As it happened, Jack was back at the checker's hut
with some five minutes to spare and within moments of
regaining our engine with the all-important can of tea,
the signal was pulled off allowing our departure. We
chuffed gently over Duddeston Road bridge, across the
main lines and on to the up goods, to proceed at a
leisurely pace to Bromford sidings where our train of
empty hopper wagons was waiting. The shunter was ready
for us and pulled over the appropriate points before
calling us back on to our train. Our guard appeared a
few moments later, coupled up, announced that we had
32 wagons, and if we were fit he would advise the inspector. 'I just want to check the sanders,' said Jack, 'but
we'll be O.K. by the time you've rung out.' So saying,
he climbed down from the footplate armed with a piece of
wire and the coal pick. I already knew the drill. First
the small cork in the base of the sand box was removed to
see if the sand ran out freely. If not, then the wire
would be inserted and poked around to loosen any clogging
obstruction. The cork would be replaced, and the sand
valve in the cab operated. With a bit of luck, sand
would then be blown in a steady stream directly between
rail and wheels. Should the flow not be up to standard,
then a couple of sharp blows with the coal pick in the
area of the sand trap at the top of the delivery pipe
would generally suffice to do the trick. It was, of
course, most important to ensure that the sanders on both
sides of the engine worked simultaneously, for if only
one side functioned, then there would be a grave risk of
broken coupling rods and crank pins. Jack quickly
completed this task since none of the boxes caused any
major problems. His main concern was that it was one of
those damp days with periods of intermittent drizzle -

not a decent downpour that would wash the rails clean,
but just enough moisture to mix with the dust collected
over the preceding dry spell, and this formed a slippery
paste which certainly did not make for good adhesion.
In the past he had rolled his train back through some
trap points on an incline and did not wish to repeat
this embarrassing experience ever again. 'Set your
lamps at Class B,' he said on regaining the footplate.
'That is, one on the top of the smokebox and one on the
centre of the buffer beam.' I did as instructed and
returned to the cab with a tingle of excitement. This
was my first real road job and I wondered how I was
going to make out. Jack's earlier attitude had done
much to destroy what confidence I had in myself, but now
it was gradually building up again.

A shrill whistle focussed our attention in the
direction of the shunter's cabin, where our guard was
now calling us with an emphatic gesture. This was it
then, I thought, as I sprang to release the hand brake,
realising that the waiting was now over. Jack eased
open the regulator while I quickly closed the firehole
doors, turned up the blower and fully opened the damper.
I was now familiar with the road and knew that I would
not be overtaxed on the slightly falling gradient as far
as Water Orton, but after that I had no idea what to
expect, except that there was a goodish bank up to Nuneaton. 'Make sure that we've got the guard,' called
Jack, who now seemed to be getting edgy again. Leaning
well out, I watched our 32 wagons slowly snake from the
sidings, over the crossovers, and out of the yard. Yes,
there was the brake van, but no sign of the guard. I
wondered where the devil he was. Then a dark shape
suddenly appeared on the verandah of the brake, with a
long arm holding a piece of white paper protruding from
the side of the van and slowly waving up and down. I,
in turn, gave a quick flap or two with my wiper, a pop
on the whistle and Jack the news that he was safely on
board.

As we chugged easily along the up goods still in full
gear and with partially opened regulator, Jack turned to
me and shouted, 'You'd better get some more fire on!
They usually turn us out on the main line at Castle
Bromwich.' I bent to the task, and had the uneasy
feeling that he was closely watching every move I made.
To create the right impression, I thought that I would
try a bit of fancy stuff and bounce the shovel off the
firehole mouthpiece. This is the normal technique for

feeding the front end of a firebox with the minimum of
effort, but not really necessary on the short firebox of
a 3F. I had started to get the hang of it on previous
firing turns, but on this occasion Jack's intense scrut-
iny had put me off my stroke somewhat. What commenced as
a smart deflection to the front right corner of the box
terminated with the shovel squarely striking the edge of
the firehole and depositing ten pounds of slack and
ovoids round Jack's ankles. This did nothing to improve
his temper or my ego. 'Never mind the front. Get a good
back on,' he grumbled irritably, shaking the slack out of
his turnups. I immediately dumped half a dozen shovels
of bricquettes and ovoids in the back corners and under
the door, flipped up the bottom flap, partially closed
the top one, and turned my attention to the pressure
gauge. It had dropped back to 160lbs. per sq.in., but
now a rich black column of smoke was billowing out of the
chimney, so I felt that soon the needle would reverse its
backward movement. In those days, I was a little uncertain how much secondary air to allow through the
firedoors, and tended in consequence to err on the side
of too little rather than too much. Drivers also seemed
to favour this method, based no doubt on the old
philosophy that where there's smoke, there's fire. As
long as they could see smoke coming from the chimney,
then they could relax, happy in the knowledge that at
least their mate had not let the fire go out, no matter
what sort of mess he was making of the rest of his
duties.

'You'll have to do better than that up the bank,' was
Jack's next scathing comment. 'We're going downhill
here!' My confidence began to drain out through my boots
again. The boiler level was showing about two-thirds of
a glass, so I turned on my injector. 'Don't put it on
now. Wait until I shut off.' Half a minute later he
closed the regulator, and I repeated the operation, at
the same time dropping the bottom firedoor to eliminate
some of the smoke which had been rolling in dense volumes
from our chimney. I couldn't make up my mind whether
Jack was trying to be awkward or trying to be helpful,
but I did feel I was being robbed of all initiative and
not giving of my best. As we moved gently up to the
starter signal at Castle Bromwich, an express passenger
hauled by a Black Five flashed past. 'You'd better put
some more on now,' he said, this time in a more moderate
tone, since by now the pressure gauge needle was on the
red line and the boiler had recovered to a full glass.

I spread another ten shovelsful around the box,
concentrating as before on building up the back to the
acknowledged classical slope, and had just completed
this when we heard the points clank over and could see
that we would indeed be turned out on to the main line.
Injector off, bottom flap up, release the hand brake,
and there we were all ready to go as the signal was
pulled off. A few gentle puffs sufficed to tauten the
couplings and then, as he felt the weight of the train,
Jack jerked open the regulator. 3435 gave a little half
slip and then surged forward with a healthy bark cracking back at us from the chimney.

Wow! I thought as I watched the train curving out
over the points. I'm working on the main line at last!
We could not, of course, dawdle here and as we
accelerated to about 20m.p.h. on the slightly falling
gradient of 1 in 955, Jack suddenly almost closed the
regulator and heaved the reversing lever back to the
first notch on the three-notch rack. He then quickly
opened up the regulator to the full first valve position
and the exhaust settled down to that crisp but slightly
irregular beat that Class 3Fs give when working on a
shortened cut-off. I glanced in the firebox and was
glad to see that it was beginning to take on that white
furnace glow. The smoke had now thinned to a light grey
and the needle had not left the red line. As our speed
increased, I was also happy to find that I had no
difficulty in keeping my balance, but then of course
Class 3s always did ride well, so I relaxed for a few
moments to enjoy the now-familiar scenery rolling past,
even though it was shrouded in mist and drizzle. Our
quick burst of effort was soon over, for the Water Orton
Junction distant signal was against us, causing Jack to
close the regulator, drop her into full gear and start
checking our speed. I put my injector on and joined
Jack on his side of the footplate so as to be in a
better position to sight the home signal over that long
sweeping righthand curve. We saw it come off just
before it was obscured by the smoke and steam from a
fast-approaching fitted on the down main. This must
have been the cause of our check, since it had no doubt
travelled over the fast at the station junction and had
consequently crossed our intended path. We were still
rolling at a reasonable rate and Jack allowed us to
continue coasting steadily towards the station junction
where we would divert to the right along what was known
as the slow. This is a loop some three miles in length

taking in Coleshill and Whitacre and rejoining the fast
again at Kingsbury Station Junction. Two miles from
Water Orton the track again diverts to the right at
Whitacre Junction, where it then proceeds through
Nuneaton, Hinckley and on to Leicester.

The distant for the station junction indicated that
we now had a clear path, and as the facing points hove
into view I wondered what sort of reaction we would feel
crossing over them. I stayed on Jack's side of the cab
in case there was an audience on the platform, but in
this respect I was to be disappointed. We clattered
through the station and under the road bridge, the
points causing only a very slight lurch, and then I
suddenly realised as we headed for Coleshill that I had
not the faintest idea what lay ahead. I noticed a
gradient board showing that we were still going downhill
at 1 in 346, but I thought it prudent to consult Jack.
'What's it like from now on?' I shouted in his ear.
'We won't use much steam until Whitacre Junction,' he
replied. 'But after that we shall be on the collar all
the way up to just this side of Stockingford Tunnel -
about six miles. What's more,' he said, grimacing as if
recalling past unpleasant experiences, 'the steepest
part is the last two miles. You've got about two miles
to Whitacre, so fill the box up!' The safety valves
were just lifting, so it was a good opportunity to build
up a really big fire. The fresh coal would cool the box
down for a while, preventing wastage of steam and
obviating the possibility of over-filling the boiler by
excessive use of the injectors. As I spread more fuel
on the only partially burned mass already in the firebox, I did not realise that I was building myself a
whole heap of trouble. One can get away with charging a
firebox if one has good quality coal such as South
Kirkby Yorkshire hard. Nicely broken and properly
applied, it will eventually burn through and give a
glorious fire providing no excessive demands are made on
the boiler during the initial stages. However, with a
mixture of bricquettes, ovoids and slack, heavy firing
merely blocks all air spaces, causing the fire to become
dead; and the fuel sets into a spongy mass that only an
energetic attack with the fireirons can break up.

By the time we arrived at Whitacre Junction, I had
all the makings of such a mass in the box, and the only
silver lining to this particular black cloud was that it
was lying on the top of a substantial amount of well
burned through fire. Signal checks had slowed us to

about 10m.p.h. on passing over the junction but, as soon
as we had cleared this, Jack brought the gear lever back
to the first notch and opened up the regulator to full
first valve. Once again that distinctive raucous blast
crashed out across the countryside as we started to
tackle the 1 in 146 towards Shustoke and up to Arley,
the location of the well-known north Warwickshire
collieries. Once again an impressive column of black
smoke rocketed skywards and then hung like a curtain in
the calm, damp air.

The scenery here was very lovely, the track running
between steep, heavily wooded banks of every shade of
green imaginable, but my mind was on other things and I
groaned inwardly at the sight of the pressure gauge
needle dropping like a stone. I couldn't believe it.
A whacking great fire in the box, clouds of black smoke
from the chimney, but the pressure falling back! The
explanation was simple, but my ignorance was such at the
time that I did not realise that the layer of fresh fuel
was acting as a screen and blanketing the heat of the
fire beneath from the rest of the box. Until that layer
became incandescent, the needle could only go one way.

With the train now on the 1 in 206 section of the
bank just past Shustoke, Jack became aware of the falling pressure as the exhaust beat took on a more laboured
note, and flashed me a look of disapproval as he dropped
the lever into full gear. 'You'd better pull the rake
through that lot,' he yelled. I started to scramble
over the tender but his hand grabbed my jacket and
pulled me back to the footplate. 'Wait until we get
through this next bridge,' he shouted in my ear, 'or
you'll knock your silly head off.' Gosh! In my anxiety
to comply I had not thought of that, for there was no
doubt I might have received a nasty injury had I come
into contact with that particular piece of ironwork,
even though our speed was now only some 15m.p.h. or so.
Jack's stature promptly jumped a couple of points in my
estimation. As the clouds of acrid smoke which had
bounced down from the bridge cleared, I once again set
off over the tender to obtain the rake. Our steam
pressure had by now dropped to under 150lbs. per sq.in.
and the water was showing about two-thirds of a glass
when, with only the top flap of the firedoors open, I
inserted the rake. The technique was to draw this
implement through the fire, starting at the front end.

It was hard, hot work and I had completed five of the
six strokes necessary, when 3435 slipped. Due to our

falling pressure, Jack had edged the regulator on to the
second valve, and as she started to slip he snapped the
regulator shut. However, it had become gagged, this
being the term used when, although the regulator handle
is in the closed position, the actual valves have not
properly shut and steam is still being admitted to the
cylinders. It was quite a common occurrence, and many
drivers developed the habit of fully opening the regulator before slamming it shut as a precaution.

This slip was a real beauty. An explosive roar
erupted from the chimney, spewing a mighty column of
steam, smoke and blazing cinders high into the air,
while the wheels revolved at an incredible speed causing
a most disconcerting up and down oscillation. I had
been on slipping engines before, but this one seemed to
go on and on, and I clung desperately to the rake which
was still buried deep in the fire. Meanwhile Jack had
acted with commendable alacrity, flicking the sand valve
open and applying the brake almost in one movement.
Now, the official instructions point out quite clearly
that the sanders should not be operated until slipping
has stopped, since the sudden shock of regaining
adhesion could cause considerable damage to the motion,
but it was common practice to take advantage of the few
seconds time lag between opening the valve and when the
sand actually began to run, so that they would be operating at full flow as soon as the regulator was reopened.
The brake application, of course, also helped to slow
the spinning wheels. Because the regulator had gagged,
Jack was obliged fully to open it before again slamming
it shut and this action not only prolonged the slip but
momentarily made it more violent. I was still hanging
on to the rake, with my face quite close to the boiler
front, when this frantic blast of energy finally ceased.
Instantly a great orange tongue of flame flared out
through the firehole into the cab. I instinctively
leaped back, but not before the major part of my
eyebrows and eyelashes had disappeared in a quick puff
of smoke. This was my first close-up of a blow back,
and I didn't like it. In fact it impressed me to such
an extent as to ingrain a lasting respect for this
phenomenon, which I always tried to anticipate and avoid.
The cause on this occasion was due to the mixing of
unburned fuel and hot fire by my efforts with the rake,
followed by a tremendous blast for a few seconds which
liberated great quantities of gases. This was quite all
right as long as they were being drawn at high velocity

through the fire tubes, but with the abrupt removal of
this powerful draught they had to escape in some direction, and the line of least resistance was into the cab.
Jack had the regulator open again even as the flames
rolled out of the firehole and, having contrived very
successfully to shrink his rotund form into that small
corner between gear lever and spectacle plate, suffered
nothing worse than a pair of over-heated trousers. With
a steady stream of sand under the wheels 3435 once more
regained her feet and settled to the struggle up the
bank which had steepened to 1 in 136.

Having decided that it was now safe, I withdrew the
red-hot rake, and quickly swung it up on the tender.
That prodigious slip had certainly done the fire a lot
of good for the needle, having hit an all-time low of
140, had now crept up to the 150 mark. The water, on
the other hand, was down to less than half a glass and I
glanced enquiringly at Jack. 'Better put it on,' he
shouted, indicating the injector. I did so, and was
delighted to find that the needle was still slowly
recovering. My spirits also rose with it, and I felt a
distinct quickening of the pulse as I listened to that
rough crisp bark as we hammered our way up to Arley and
Fillongly station. Jack was operating the sanding gear
intermittently, more as a precaution than a necessity,
but what a good job, I thought, that he had checked
their efficiency before starting. A little bit of
forethought and a thorough knowledge of the road made
life so much easier on the footplate when properly
applied.

With 160 on the clock and the water an inch below the
top nut, I dropped the firedoor with the intention of
shooting a quick half-dozen around the box. I bent to
grasp the shovel only to find that Jack had hauled up
the flap again. 'Don't do it like that,' he yelled.
'Fire it over the flap. Like this,' he continued,
brushing me aside, for I had greeted this remark with a
look of blank amazement. He scooped up a level shovelful of slack, and with the handle held at a high angle,
sprayed the fuel mixture in over the bottom door. He
repeated the operation some six times in quick
succession, thrust the shovel into my hands and shouted,
'Carry on then. You can fire almost continuously like
that while we're working hard.' I looked first at the
pressure gauge which was still showing 160 and then at
the water which was just in sight, and decided there and
then that this could be the right answer. In actual

fact, I found that this was indeed an excellent method
of firing an engine fitted with the old Midland type
doors, providing that conditions warranted it. That is
to say, if the engine was working hard, and the fuel was
of a small size. A steam-shy engine does not like a lot
of cold air going into its firebox and this was a very
good way of keeping it down to a minimum. The draught
drew the fuel off the shovel, and by skilful angling of
the blade, the whole box could be evenly fired.

We were now more than halfway up the bank, and I was
being kept pretty busy, for with the regulator on full
first valve and the gear lever at maximum cut-off, fuel
was disappearing into that white-hot slot as fast as I
could shovel it. Through Arley and Fillongly the
gradient eases slightly from 1 in 132 to 1 in 240 and,
as our pace quickened, so our exhaust beat became
crisper and more strident. I began to feel for the first
time that complex mixture of emotion which was, in the
course of time, to provide the ultimate sense of satisfaction when working a steam locomotive.

Between Arley and Fillongly station and Arley colliery
sidings is the steepest part of the bank at 1 in 109.
With only two miles to go to the summit I was beginning
to think that I had mastered this new technique of
firing, for the pressure gauge was showing 170lbs. per
sq.in. and the water was just in sight at the top of the
glass. Even Jack seemed less tense, and as we crashed
our way up past the colliery, he took the trouble to
point out the position of his dreaded catch-points. I
watched these clatter by under our wheels, and then
glanced up at the pressure gauge for reassurance. My
heart missed half a dozen beats as I blinked disbeliev-
ingly at it. The needle was dropping steadily and was
already pointing at 160lbs. per sq.in. Now what had
gone wrong? I said to myself as I quickly shut off the
injector. I just could not think what might have caused
this dramatic fall. The glare from the slot seemed as
bright as ever, but the smoke at the chimney had thinned
considerably. I re-doubled my efforts with the shovel
and poured in more fuel. I was surprised to find that
not as much smoke was being generated as before and,
moreover, the needle had not stopped its downward swing.
As the sound of the blast lost some of its former bite,
Jack pulled his head in from round the side of the cab
to investigate the cause. His voice now had a definite
tinge of excitement in it and rose a couple of octaves
in consequence as he eyed the gauge which had halted at

145lbs. per sq.in. 'I can't ease up yet,' he screeched.
'We're the wrong side of the catch-points to stick,' and
he pushed the regulator over on to the second valve as
if to emphasise his statement. 'What have you done?
What have you done?' He repeated this question three or
four times while hopping up and down on his platform.
'I don't know,' I mumbled truthfully, while ruminating
how amazingly light on their feet fat men could be.
Finally the hopping ceased and Jack, having grabbed the
shovel, made a quick inspection of the firebox by using
its blade as a deflector. 'You've choked it under the
arch,' he announced in a sour voice, snapping shut both
firedoors. 'Get the rake down and pull it back, for
heaven's sake, and be quick about it!' he said as he
hopped back on to his platform.
    As I wrestled the rake into the firebox again, I
noted that the pressure had, if anything, risen slightly
but the water level was steadily dropping. This time
raking was much worse than before, since for one thing
the surface of the fire was hotter and for another, a
great many more than six strokes were required. The
space underneath the brick arch was blocked by a mass of
small, burning particles of fuel, which had arrived
there by the action of the blast taking them from a
shovel held at the wrong angle. I should have held the
handle higher, so that the coal entered the box close
to the firedoors instead of halfway to the front.
Vibration had also assisted in shaking the fire forward,
with the ovoids rolling downhill, and the result was a
shape exactly opposite to what was desired and a typical
consequence of over-enthusiasm and lack of experience.
My arms ached so much that I could hardly move them and
the rake was too hot to hold anyhow, so with a last
desperate effort I hauled the glowing implement from
the fire and swung it on to the tender. I was momentarily exhausted, but at least the needle was once again
travelling in the right direction, evidence that I had
been partially successful in clearing the blockage.
'Get some water in the boiler,' shouted Jack.
'Otherwise we'll drop a plug when we go over the top.'
We were by then only about half a mile from the summit
and from climbing at 1 in 125 we would abruptly start
descending at 1 in 168, increasing to 1 in 126. Two
inches of water in the glass would disappear from sight
as soon as the boiler tilted downwards. I did not fully
appreciate what Jack meant, but I had already learned to
act first and ask for an explanation afterwards, so I

put my injector on, somewhat relieved to see that the
steam pressure had recovered to 155lbs. per sq.in. I
then asked what he meant about dropping a plug. In a
few brief sentences which contained more choice adject-
ives than I had heard in the whole of my life, he
explained. Practical lessons like these are so much
better learned on the footplate than in the classroom.

That last half-mile with the gallant old lady
blasting away on second valve was an anxious period for
both of us. She wasn't steaming well enough to leave
the injector on all the time so it was a case of trying
to hit a compromise which would ensure sufficient water
in the boiler as we breasted the summit, and sufficient
steam pressure to get us there. Not quite knowing how
far we had to go was a great handicap for me, so I had
to rely entirely on Jack's judgment and this, even in
his excited condition, was logically to sacrifice water
for steam pressure initially and then, as we approached
the summit, allow the water to build up at the expense
of steam. Fortunately, 3435 was game to the last puff
and, although we struggled over the summit with only
135lbs. per sq.in. on the clock, we had two inches of
water in sight when the regulator was closed. It had
been a close thing, far closer than I realised, for a
slip like our previous one would no doubt have brought
us to a stand from which we would have had great difficulty in getting into motion again, not without a blow up
to regain a full head of steam anyway.

Jack visibly relaxed as we rolled gently down towards
the rather foreboding black maw of the 995-yard Arley
Tunnel. 'Screw the hand brake on, mate,' he said quite
affably. 'It's downhill all the way to Nuneaton now,
and we want to keep the train buffered up.' He applied
the steam brake, enabling me to get a good bite,
knocked the blower fully open, and then with what might
be construed as a grin said, 'Don't forget to keep your
head in. It's wet and smelly in here, and keep the doors
boxed up and the blower on.' I had not been through a
tunnel of this length before and wondered what it would
be like. As the darkness closed over us I noted that the
steam pressure was recovering nicely and there was certainly plenty of room in the boiler so I could safely
leave the injector on. We of course wanted as much
pressure as possible to ensure braking efficiency, but
we certainly did not want the safety valves blowing off
in the tunnel. With the firedoors closed and no gauge
lamp lit, the blackness was virtually complete. I tried

holding my hand in front of my face by way of experiment
and, not being able to see a thing, groped my way to the
tender. The air was certainly smelly. It had a stale
acrid flavour, which I found in due course was typical
of a great many tunnels and, since breathing became more
difficult, concluded that it was low in oxygen content.
I looked up in an endeavour to view the tunnel lining,
but after receiving an eyeful of dirty water, decided
nothing was to be gained by this notion and returned
unsteadily to my seat. We rumbled on, every sound being
greatly amplified in the confines of the tunnel, while
Jack kept our speed in check by regular applications of
the steam brake. I wondered how he managed to gauge our
speed so accurately while not being able to see a thing,
and then I noticed a small circle of light far ahead.
It was so clear and perfectly formed that at first I did
not recognise it for what it was - the end of the tunnel.
This circle steadily grew in area and intensity until
at last we were out into broad daylight once more. I
took a deep breath of fresh air and felt relieved that
I could again see everything on the footplate. The
pressure was back to 170lbs per sq.in. and the water was
showing three-quarters of a glass. On observing this
check, Jack, now quite cheerful, responded with, 'We'll
roll all the way to Abbey Street, so you can tidy up and
put some water in the bucket for a wash.'
    Not wishing the relieving fireman to see the uneven-
ness of the fire, I once again got busy with the rake
and pulled the remains of the heap under the arch back
to quite a respectable shape. Satisfied with this, I
then cleared the spillage from the footboards and
dropped it into the back corners of the firebox, leaving
the doors open so as not to generate too much steam.
A quick swish round with the slaking pipe soon had the
rest of the dust and debris washed overboard and the
footplate was transformed to a very presentable appearance. All through my career I could never understand
why some men seemed content to hand over an engine in a
deplorable condition, when only a few seconds' work with
brush and slaking pipe could give it that scrubbed deck
look. I could forgive a chap for having a dirty fire,
no coal brought forward, low steam pressure and a half-
empty boiler, but never a dirty footplate. Jack managed
to complete his ablutions by setting the steam brake on
a partial application which, together with the tender
brake still operating, kept our speed in check on the
1 in 135 gradient. In true oriental custom I had second

dip in the bucket and had just finished as we approached
Abbey Street station, where we rumbled gently to a halt
at the water column at the far end of the up platform.
Our relief crew, two senior Leicester men, were already
walking over to us as we collected our kit together, and
we exchanged the usual pleasantries and information
about our respective engines and trains. The one we
were to take back to Birmingham was standing across the
line on the down loop, and consisted of a mixed freight
of 42 wagons headed by Class 8F 8319. 'She's a bit of a
rattlebox, but apart from that, quite all right,' said
the other driver as we bade farewell.

On climbing aboard I was glad to see that the footplate had been left in a clean and tidy condition, also
that we had a good supply of 'real' coal in the tender.
The boiler was nearly full, whilst the firebox contained
a substantial bed of well-burned through fuel. It looked
somewhat dead, but this was because both dampers were in
the shut position. Jack pulled his watch from his
waistcoat pocket. 'We usually follow the slow,' he said.
'So that gives us about forty minutes in which to have
our food.' With this announcement I suddenly realised
that I was ravenous and quickly disposed of my packet of
sandwiches, while I watched with increasing fascination
Jack's preparations for his lunch. His generously
proportioned abdomen should have indicated to me that he
was an enthusiastic trencherman but it wasn't until I
saw the quantity and variety of food he brought out from
his haversack that the point went home. It soon became
obvious that he was very experienced in the art of footplate gastronomics and quickly transformed the cab of
that 8F into a makeshift kitchen in which he performed
his tasks with the accomplished ease of a hotel chef.

First he heated the firing shovel by placing the
blade just inside the mouthpiece ring. This was then
blasted spotlessly clean with a jet of steam and water
from the slaking pipe. Several large rashers of best
streaky bacon were placed on the blade and quickly
fried, again by holding it just inside the mouthpiece.
When cooked to his satisfaction, these were removed and
placed on three enormous slices of bread laid out for
the purpose. He next dropped a knob of butter into the
hot shovel and added a good handful of button mushrooms
and, although I had just eaten, the smell soon had my
mouth watering. The mushrooms were added to the bacon
and these in turn were followed by three fried eggs.
Finally some tomatoes were fried, and the resulting pulp

poured over the whole treat, whilst so as not to waste
the residual fat in the shovel a further round of bread
was fried. Any one of those three open sandwiches would
have satisfied the average man but Jack, having gobbled
them down at an astonishing speed, seemed almost
disappointed that there were no more. Looking up for
the first time after starting this feast, he actually
grinned broadly. 'By jingoes, I feel better for that,'
he exclaimed, reaching out for the tea can, quite
oblivious that I had watched every move. Footplate
fry-ups, I discovered later, were quite commonplace with
many drivers, but I was never again booked with anyone
who was able to cook such a variety and quantity of
food, so quickly and with such skill.

A semi-fitted hauled by a new-looking 4F 0-6-0
clattered past on the down main, and could be heard for
some considerable time snorting heavily as it laboured
up the bank towards Stockingford Tunnel. 'The slow will
be along in about ten minutes,' said Jack, 'so I'd open
the rear damper and get the fire warmed up if I were
you.' I turned the blower on slightly and pulled up the
lefthand damper, somewhat surprised to find that he was
now advising me rather than telling me what to do. Had
the breakfast worked the miracle, or had he more confidence in me now? I could not decide, but I certainly
preferred this new attitude. 'I've never worked an 8F
on a train before,' I said a little apprehensively,
thinking that this pronouncement might cause a reversion
to his former self. 'Don't worry, lad, we shouldn't
have much trouble with this little lot. We've bags of
power and they're good steamers, but you'll probably
have trouble reaching the front when we're on the move,
so bang some up there now and just keep the back damper
open.' I took up the shovel, still shining from its
recent culinary episode. It was of the long-handled
type and, as one might expect, ideally suited to the
long firebox and roomy cab of a Class 8. Firing shovels
came in two sizes, long-handled and short. Engines with
short, steeply sloping fireboxes such as 2Fs, 3Fs and
4Fs did not require a powerful swing to fire the front
of the box. This was just as well since these engines
had small cabs, making such an action difficult.
Although some tank engines, such as 2-6-4 passenger
tanks, had rather larger boxes, their cab layout again
prevented a lengthy swing, and the short-handled type
was generally preferred. However, on most of the larger
tender locomotives and indeed all the B.R. Standard

engines, long-handled ones were most suitable, and you
soon noticed the difference if supplied with the wrong
type.

With a great deal of concentration and a lot of
wasted energy I managed to place a suitable quantity of
coal in the front half of the firebox and was just hanging my head out of the side window for a breather when a
Compound hauling six coaches rolled briskly past and
came to a halt in the station. This must be the slow, I
thought, and turned to Jack for confirmation. He nodded.
'Right, you can build up the back now,' he said, knocking the blower wide open and winding the gear lever down
to the full forward position. I quickly plied more coal
to the back half of the grate and had just closed the
firedoors to the halfway position when a shrill whistle
from the station indicated that the slow was about to
depart. I hurried over to my window to watch it pull
out. It blasted away in fine style for a few yards,
then went into a spectacular slip, shooting up a plume
of smoke and steam while its 7' drivers clattered round
at a fearsome rate. Then with sanders on, it settled
down and its healthy, crisp exhaust could be heard
accelerating away as it attached the bank, working on
simple engine. Compounds were usually very quiet
exhaust-wise, when compounding, but were as crisp as any
other Midland engine when working on simple. As that
thrilling sound died away in the distance, I once more
turned my attention to the state of our own locomotive.
Steam pressure was on the 220lbs. per sq.in. mark, the
water just in sight at the top of the glass, and the
fire was burning up brightly. It seemed an awful lot
more engine than the little 3F and I felt more than a
little excited at the prospect of working her back to
Saltley.

The points clattered over and Jack applied the steam
brake. 'Take the hand brake off, mate,' he called and,
as he opened the small injector, so the signal controlling our siding dropped. Jack eased open the regulator
and after a few revolutions of the wheels, closed the
taps. We clanked slowly out on to the main line. One
of the cylinder cocks on my side was obviously sticking,
since each stroke of the piston was accompanied by a
powerful hiss from the outlet pipe. Also both piston
glands were blowing moderately, which was a further
indication that she had run up a fair mileage since her
last shopping. I put the live steam injector on in
order to prevent blowing off as we trundled through the

station, but now the starter showed that we had the road
and Jack hauled open the regulator. The exhaust
suddenly became audible as a deep-throated, slightly
muffled woof, the hisses at the front end became louder
and more penetrating while a very distinct thump could
be felt through the footboards once every revolution.
With the cab doors open, I leaned out of the driver's
side in order to make sure that the train was intact and
that the guard was in his van. Having exchanged hand
signals with him, I advised Jack, who merely nodded and
opened the regulator to about full first valve. The
exhaust crashed out, a much deeper full-bodied sound
than the 3F, and Jack wound back the reversing screw
two or three turns. As he did so, the thump from below
took on a new dimension, just as though a steam hammer
was attacking the underside of the footboards. I was
fascinated to watch the tea can leap about half an inch
clear of the drip tray at each mighty blow. Jack
scowled, partially closed the regulator and wound the
screw down a couple of turns. The violence subsided
somewhat. 'Crikey,' he commented. 'She's a bit rough.
Can't pull her up much, that's for sure!' I later
learned that should the big ends of an engine be worn
to such an extent as to produce a powerful knock, then
the condition became progressively worse the wider the
regulator was opened, and the shorter the cut-off used.
Worn big ends usually went along with worn everything
else, looseness in the axleboxes, etc., and conditions
on the footplate particularly at speed could be quite
intolerable if the engine was worked normally. By using
a smaller regulator opening and longer cut-off it was
possible to smooth out some of the bangs, rattles and
thumps, so making life a little less of a misery. Even
so, on many occasions I have found it quite impossible
to sit down while an engine was in motion.

We clumped and clanged our way back up the 1 in 123
gradient from Abbey Street with little apparent effort
and, since the safety valves were beginning to lift, I
opened the firedoors and commenced shovelling. I was
not very adept in those early days at firing from the
righthand side, but with an 8F there is quite sufficient
room in the cab to stand behind the driver and still get
a good swing with a long-handled shovel, provided that
the tender doors are not open. My attempts to reach the
front of the grate were not altogether successful, since
when I put all possible effort behind the swing I tended
to lose direction and occasionally struck the mouthpiece

ring. Apart from the damage to my ego, I received a
stinging shock through the full length of my right arm
and coal ricocheted all round the cab like so much
shrapnel. However, the 8F was very tolerant as to where
the coal was placed in the grate, and the needle barely
left the red line even when I used the exhaust injector.
Another very noticeable difference between the 8F and
the 3F was that because of the greater boiler capacity,
one travelled much farther before there was a marked
drop in the boiler water level. This, together with its
excellent steaming qualities, did much to restore my
confidence, which had sunk so low earlier in the day.
Jack also seemed more confident and relaxed, and even
indulged in some idle gossip when climbing towards the
tunnel. As we thumped our way steadily up the 1 in 126
gradient, he turned to me and shouted, 'We've only got
about a mile to go before we reach the summit, so you
needn't fire her any more. We don't want to choke
ourselves going through Arley Tunnel, and we'll need
steam on this time. We're O.K. now,' he added, indicating the full boiler and the pressure gauge still showing
225lbs. per sq.in., 'and you'll want some room to stop
her blowing off down the bank.' By this, of course, he
meant that it was good policy to work the boiler level
down somewhat so that the injector could be used when
coasting to prevent wasting steam by blowing off, without
the risk of overfilling the boiler.

I was initially doubtful whether we could travel that
far without further attention to the engine's needs but
as we approached those massive stone portals, the water
was still showing two-thirds of a glass. I was amazed
at the reserve capacity of an 8F when compared to the
small engines I had been used to. Once more the inky
blackness closed over us, and the pounding exhaust
reverberated from the tunnel walls, partially masking
the amplified clank of side rods. This time we left the
firedoors slightly open so that a shaft of intense white
light illuminated the clouds of steam that billowed
round the rear of the cab. As we penetrated farther
into the tunnel, the atmosphere became progressively
more foul, and acrid smoke fumes began to irritate our
lungs. Obviously the Compound had not been so meticulous about emitting smoke when passing through. I
squeezed myself as far as possible into the front corner
of the cab, and watched with fascination the flow of
steam and smoke as it poured round the trailing edge of
the roof and moved in a succession of jerks corresponding

to the exhaust beats towards the firedoors. I had
always imagined that it would travel in a steady flow.
Suddenly the noise subsided as we burst out into daylight. I quickly slid forward the side window and hung
my head out, taking in gulps of fresh air while I
observed the vast cloud of steam and smoke which rolled
upwards over the tunnel mouth - sucked out by the motion
of our train.

Jack closed the regulator and, without being told
this time, I put the exhaust injector on. Despite being
on a downgrade of 1 in 125 the water was still showing
a third of a glass and the safety valves were just
beginning to lift, but I now had plenty of boiler room
to keep her quiet. Kicking the firedoors open on the
way, I moved in anticipation over to the hand brake.
'Yes, wind it on a bit, mate,' he said, seemingly
pleased that I had been alert to this intended
manoeuvre. We now had five miles of downhill coasting
to Whitacre so I studied the fire to see what mistakes
I had made. The rear half of the grate was reasonably
even and well filled, but the front half was just the
opposite. Humps and ridges were interspersed with
valleys and depressions where the fire was so thin that
holes were beginning to form. I quickly realised that
there was a lot to be learned about this firing
business, particularly when physical strength had to be
combined with skill and accuracy.

As our speed increased under the influence of
gravity, a peculiar buffeting motion set up between the
engine and tender, which was only checked when Jack made
a steady application of the steam brake. It was decidedly unpleasant, but had the advantage of tending to
shake down coal ready for use on the tender shovelling
plate. I cocked an enquiring eyebrow in Jack's
direction. 'Weak springs, I reckon,' he muttered by
way of explanation. I sat down on my seat, which on a
Class 8 is merely a spring-loaded wooden flap, listening
contentedly to the rhythmic clanking of the motion and
the whistle of air through the jammed exhaust cocks, and
reflecting that nearly all sounds from a steam locomotive are very beautiful sounds - even when they indicate
a fault.

Our descent of the bank was uneventful and I was
able to repair the fire at leisure with fresh coal,
filling in the holes which had formed. By leaving the
firedoors wide open, I was able to prevent generating
excessive smoke as the coal ignited; at the same time

the cooling effect of the secondary air prevented
blowing off. My intention was to arrive at Whitacre
with a full boiler and a bright fire, ready for a quick
dash to Washwood Heath. However, when all too soon the
Whitacre Junction distant became visible against its
backcloth of bright May greenery, it was seen to be on.
Jack brought our speed right down on the still-falling
gradient of 1 in 146, with lengthy applications of the
brake, and as we hissed and clanked up to the home
signal we could see that a local trip engine was drawing
out of the down sidings. We waited a few moments before
being allowed to draw up to the starter and then, after
a further interval of some ten minutes or so when the
trip engine had cleared Coleshill, we were allowed to
proceed. I had filled the boiler well above the top of
the gauge glass, but even so, Jack was able to use such
a small regulator opening in getting our train moving up
the 1 in 735 gradient to Coleshill that no trace of
priming was noticeable.

We did in fact reach Water Orton station junction,
two miles farther on, before the water came into sight
again, where once more we were brought to a halt while a
mixed freight passed in front of us from the down fast
on to the slow. Our signals indicated that we were also
to travel up the slow and, just as we hissed gently to a
stand at Water Orton Junction home signal, so it too
came off. As we clanked towards the signal box, a green
flag was thrust out of the nearest side window and, on
spotting this, Jack reached up and gave a short hoot on
the whistle. We still called them whistles on a Class 8,
but the instruments fitted by Sir William to his locomotives were pitched (acoustically speaking) rather low,
and tended most of the time to sound like an asthmatic
bullfrog. Hence, while the term 'croaker' might have
been more accurate, it never caught on, nor for that
matter did 'hooter', so 'whistle' it was. I always felt
that the timbre and pitch of a whistle should suit the
size and characteristics of the engine it was attached
to. For example, the shrill, clear bell-like tones of a
3F were very appropriate, and very feminine. The deep-
throated hoot of the larger Stanier engines was again in
keeping with their size, power and masculinity, whilst
the high-pitched piping of a B.R. Class 9F seemed
absolutely ridiculous - a giant with a midget's voice.
Nothing less than an ocean-going liner's siren would
have satisfied me for this magnificent piece of
locomotive engineering. That they were so equipped

seems all the more a pity since the Riddles design team
experimented with whistles in their early days, and
fitted a beautiful triple-tone chime whistle to the
Standard Class 5. We all thought these a wonderful
novelty, and I recall continually playing 'tunes' on
them at every opportunity. Even the most staid of the
senior drivers seemed to be bitten with the same bug and,
when only moving around the shed yard, managed to give a
pretty good impersonation of the Santa Fe Express.
Maybe this was one reason why the idea was abandoned,
apart from cost.

On passing the junction signal box we waved to the
bobby, who held up two fingers. I thought that this was
a rather unfriendly gesture, and was about to reply in a
like manner, when Jack grunted, 'There's two in front of
us then.' I asked him to explain, and was it anything
to do with the green flag business? It seems that this
was another instance of permissive block working, which
allowed two or more trains to be on the same section of
track at the same time providing that the crews had been
properly advised. This only applied to the goods line,
but it did mean that a great number of trains could be
accommodated on that four-mile stretch between Water
Orton Junction and Washwood Heath Junction. In the
early 1950s it was by no means an uncommon sight to see
it full from end to end with waiting trains. I have
personally relieved a train at Castle Bromwich and have
been relieved again eight hours later at Washwood Heath,
having travelled less than two miles during that period.
No wonder this condition was known to all as 'on the
block'. The two fingers had indicated the number of
trains in front of us on the section to Castle Bromwich,
a useful tip when visibility was bad.

We chugged steadily along the goods line, keeping an
eye open for the brake van of the preceding train. The
drizzle had now stopped and the sky was brightening
considerably, making the lush grass in the meadows to
our left look greener than ever. We found only one
train in front of us at the Castle Bromwich home
signals, and this was allowed to proceed after we had
halted for only a short while. Ten minutes later we
followed suit, again being advised by the bobby that we
were in a queue. This time we moved only at walking
pace, since the goods line curves round the back of the
down platform at Castle Bromwich station before passing
under the Chester Road bridge and forward vision is
severely limited. On clearing that road bridge, we saw

that the now-familiar brake of the train ahead was only
a hundred yards away but apparently still on the move,
judging by the little puffs of steam, like so many balls
of cotton wool, rising lazily into the air from above
the line of wagon roofs. We crept forward like this for
a few hundred yards and then came to a standstill for
half an hour. This was followed by another few hundred
yards of movement and then a further halt. It was about
this time I realised that, although an 8F has many
advantages over a 3F, the seating layout was certainly
not one of them. Providing that one had a suitable piece
of wood on a 3F, one could quickly arrange a very
comfortable couch and a pleasant forty winks might
follow. The one-foot square flap seat on an 8F did not
allow any more relaxed an attitude than sitting upright,
and my legs were too short to even reach the footboards
comfortably. I could achieve a sort of reclining
position by putting my feet up on the drip tray or the
tops of the damper handles but since my legs were just
about at full stretch, they tended to slip off as soon
as the muscles relaxed. Unless I was desperately tired
not even a light doze was possible.

While I was still contemplating this shortcoming in
the 8F design features, Jack again drew out his watch,
studied it with his usual care and then turned to me
with a smile and said, 'Well, mate, at least we won't
have to put her away. We're on overtime now.' I had
not realised that it was more than eight hours since
booking on and, now that our official day was up, we
would not have to dispose of our engine even if we went
straight to the shed. Not that there was much hope of
that, since there was still another train in front of us
before we reached Bromford Bridge station home signals.
Forty minutes later found us under the station starter
signal, and I had just changed my seating position for
the 49th time when a friendly voice called to us from
the trackside. 'Hold on, we're after you.' I opened
the cab doors on Jack's side and a relief crew from the
control link climbed on board. Greetings and information
were rapidly exchanged and both Jack and I, now feeling
the need for further refreshment, grabbed our respective
empty lunch bags and set off to hoof the two miles or so
to Saltley shed. We were allowed fifty minutes walking
time from Bromford, but Jack was not disposed to walking
any more than was strictly necessary. Not that he could
be blamed on this particular jaunt, since clumping over
ballast, sleepers, point rods, signal wires and general

bric-a-brac for more than two miles was certainly
unpleasant. The official and correct route lay through
the slum streets of east Birmingham, but even on a
bright May afternoon such a journey brought no sense of
pleasure.

Fortunately the train in front started to move as we
reached the ground and I was amazed at Jack's speed and
agility as he bounded after that retreating brake van.
Needless to say, I was close on his heels as he tumbled
inelegantly on to the van's verandah but, as he so
rightly observed, a bad ride was better than a good walk.
By hopping from one train to another we managed to get
to the West End in reasonable time, from where even Jack
was able to stroll to the loco without too much distress.
As we entered the enginemen's lobby, I noticed an
unusually large crowd of chaps jostling around the
notice board. 'What's all the excitement about?' I
enquired of a Passed Cleaner colleague who was standing
nearby. 'We've been registered now,' he said, grinning
from ear to ear as he swelled with pride. 'You're
booked with Ronnie Jackson,' he added, pointing to the
lists of links. 'Nice chap. I was with him last week.'

There it was then, in black and white: 'Washwood
Heath link. Driver.R.Jackson. Fireman.T.Essery.' A
full-blown fireman at last. But who was this Ronnie
Jackson? No matter, I would find out at 2.00 p.m.
Monday afternoon, for that was the time scheduled to
book on for disposal work.

IV

THE FIRST RUNG OF THE LADDER

1.30 p.m. on Monday afternoon found me racing over
the cobbled sets of Duddeston Mill Road on my trusty
bicycle, before charging up the slope across the shed
forecourt and through the car park to drop it into a
vacant slot in the cycle racks. On my first day as a
registered fireman, I had no intention of being late,
for I still had to find out what driver Jackson looked
like. I entered the enginemen's lobby more confidently
than ever before, feeling that I was now part of the
elite. Drawing my card from Peter the clerk, I asked if
Ronnie Jackson had booked on yet. Peter glanced at the
clock. 'Good lord, not yet,' he said. 'You're a bit
early, you know. He'll be in, though, about five to
two.' 'Give me the tip when he arrives,' I said over my
shoulder as I moved off to read the notice boards.

Another of the lads I had been cleaning with bowled
in full of exuberance and also nearly half an hour early,
so we soon became engrossed in relating our exploits
since passing out. Whilst still deep in conversation, I
felt a tap on my shoulder, and on turning found myself
confronted by a chubby, baby-faced driver in his early
thirties. His rosy round features were split by a
cheerful grin, and I noticed with growing approval a
deeply dimpled chin and twinkling blue eyes. 'Are you
Terry Essery?' he said. I nodded. 'You must be Ronnie
Jackson.' 'That's right,' he said, 'Let's go round to
the cabin and get acquainted.' The cabin to which he
referred was a large cavernous room located under the
water tank adjacent to Number Two shed, and served as a
mess room for enginemen until replaced by a far more
grandiose affair which was erected in the mid-1950s -
known officially as the Staff Amenities Block.

The mess room as such was not very elegant, having
high arched windows (always semi-opaque), a stone-
flagged floor and zinc-topped tables with rather uncomfortable benches attached. One ancient and stained
porcelain sink, along with three more modern but equally
stained hand basins, provided the only washing
facilities, but set in the middle was a gigantic
combustion stove capable of roasting all the inhabitants
even in the depth of winter. To supplement this heating,
one wall sported an open fireplace large enough to do

justice to any baronial hall, while in the corner of the
room stood a great cast iron urn of water perpetually on
the boil. Anyhow, it was home to us and there was
always an open forum running where many and varied
subjects were hotly debated. What was going to win the
3.30 at Cheltenham, the merits of Beethoven's piano
sonatas or the state of the fireirons on the disposal
pits, could all crop up in five minutes flat.

Ron had collected a tea can from his locker on the
way to the mess room, and as we entered he suggested we
had a cup of tea first. The mashing operation completed,
he guided me to a quiet corner and when comfortably
seated, opened a most enlightening conversation. 'O.K.,
mate,' he said. 'You've got a lot to learn, so we might
as well start off by giving you an idea of what happens
in the link. As you probably know, we are mainly
concerned with the preparation and disposal of engines
on the shed, with the odd bit of marshalling thrown in.
We used to have some shunting turns as well, but these
have been taken over by diesels now, so it's unlikely
that we will ever go past the loco signal. Now then,
since we're on disposal, I'll explain all about this
first. We operate two systems here; we can either
volunteer for the quota system, which means that each
crew has to dispose of six engines as quickly as
possible and then they are finished for the day, or we
can wait for the yard foreman to allocate engines to us
as and when required.

'The advantage of the quota system is, of course,
that it is possible to go home after four, three or even
two hours and still be paid for eight hours, but to take
full advantage of it the driver has to deal with one
engine, while the fireman takes another. Believe me, it
can be very hard work doing the lot yourself, and you
have to work without a break. You also require sufficient engines to go at, and there are certain times of
the day when very little comes on the shed, so you have
to choose the time carefully. Furthermore, the fireman
has to be sufficiently strong, skilled and trustworthy to
carry out these tasks without supervision, because if
anything goes wrong it's the driver who carries the
can.'

I conceded this point. 'Although it often suits me
to work the quota system,' he went on, 'I do not propose
to try it until we've been together for a while. For
one thing, I don't think it would be fair to you, and
for another, I would have grey hairs wondering what you

were getting up to.' 'Okay,' I replied with a smile,
since Ron said this in the nicest possible way. 'The
yard foreman will give the quota men all the available
engines first, so we'll have to wait awhile, but we
shall probably get our first one about 3.30. In the
meantime, I'll run through the procedure so that you'll
have an idea of what to expect.

'Engines are normally left on one of the two arrival
roads, that is, the ones leading under the coaling plant.
If the tanks are less than half full, then we top them
up, otherwise we don't usually bother. The foreman will
tell us whether to just clean the fire or whether to drop
it completely. This happens if the engine is required
for repairs or washing out. He will also tell us where
to stable it and if it requires turning. Normally we
coal the goods engines at the far end of the plant since
this contains the poorer grades, unless advised otherwise, and passenger engines, Black Fives and 'Crabs' at
the near end. I'll show you how to operate the plant
when the time comes. After coaling, we move down to
the ashpit, and if the road is empty we clean the fire
at the ash hopper. The road is usually full, though, so
we have to throw out the fire on the side of the pit,
but you'll see when we get there.

'When we're over the pit, you can get underneath and
rake out the ash pan, and when that's done you finally
clear the smokebox of char. I will have completed my
examination by then, so after that it's only a matter of
dropping it in the shed and returning the tools to the
stores, O.K.?' I had, of course, an idea of disposal
procedures, but I was grateful for having it spelled out
in detail.

We went on chatting in general, and we seemed to have
known each other much longer than a mere two hours when
at 3.45 p.m. one of the foreman's assistants came up to
Ron and asked him if he would care to dispose of 4203, a
4F standing on the front arrival road. 'Leave a bit in,
and drop it in Number Two shed,' he added as he moved
over to give instructions to another set of disposal men.

It was a humid day and, although a thin veil of cloud
was drawn across the sun, I could feel its heat as we
walked across to our engine. With the temperature in
the low seventies, I had visions of some warm work ahead
of us. Ron preceded me on to the footplate and his
first action was to test the water gauge. 'Always check
the water level first,' he said, 'and then make sure that
there is plenty of steam. Sometimes they arrive on shed

without much of either, in which case you have to raise
more steam and fill the boiler up. If you don't, you
may find yourself having to be towed off the pit, and
that upsets everyone.' He pulled open the firedoors,
which were of the sliding pattern, and glanced inside.
'Hmm! Looks a bit rough! still, I thought it might be,
judging by the amount of coal used. I'm going to drop
down to the water column first. We'll have to fill this
one.' As I scrambled on to the tender I noticed that
the tank gauge was showing less than a thousand gallons,
and that over two-thirds of the coal supply had been
consumed; she had obviously been out some good while.
'Throw the fireirons into the back of the tender while
you're up there, mate,' called Ron as he opened the
water column valve. I did as requested, realising that
you could not very easily coal the tender with fireirons
lying across the top of it.

While waiting for the tank to fill, I surveyed the
shed yard from my elevated position. It was certainly a
veritable hive of activity. To my front, a queue of
engines stood on both arrival roads, stretching underneath the towering, blackened concrete structure of the
coaling plant. Beyond, this queue continued right down
over the pits to the ash plant, where the engines were
obscured in a haze of smoke and dust as the quota men
did desperate battle with clinker and char. To my
right, a train of coal wagons stood waiting to deliver
their loads into the insatiable maw of the plant hopper,
and standing behind these on the back departure roads
were lines of prepared engines awaiting their crews.
Over to my left there was the busy bustle of traffic
moving into and out of the three roundhouses, while just
before me engines were leaving for unknown destinations.

A frantic gurgling from the tank indicated that it
was near to overfilling. 'O.K., Ron, that'll do,' I
yelled and, as the flow ceased, I hauled the wet,
slippery hose from the opening and pushed it aside
before replacing the lid. I had already been instructed
to make sure that the tank cover was in position before
coaling, since a hundredweight of coal going into the
water compartment every time the engine went under the
hopper would soon severely restrict its capacity, to say
nothing of the effect on the delivery pipes. Ron eased
forwards and, being a goods engine, we had to obtain our
coal from the far end, but we were unable to get into
the correct position straight away, for the queue was
still blocking us. 'I'll show you how the plant works

while we're waiting,' said Ron, as he skipped lightly on
to the concrete platform which ran the full length of the
hopper between the two roads. We entered one of the two
little concrete huts which housed the control gear.
These huts were substantial structures capable of with-
standing the impact of the heaviest lump of coal which
might bounce off an over-coaled tender and, although they
had glass windows in either side, these were protected by
heavy wire grilles.

Inside, two large metal levers mounted in slotted
quadrants - looking not unlike the reversing levers of a
Class 3F - protruded from the floor. These controlled
the angle of the delivery chutes, one for each track,
while mounted on the wall were two sets of water valves
for the sprinkler systems and two switch boxes containing
separate on and off buttons, again one set for each
track. The principle was simple: coal from the hopper
fed on to a metal plate which moved backwards and
forwards like a shuttle when the switch was pressed.
Coal dropping over the edge of this moving plate fell on
to the chute, which in turn deflected it into the tender.
The angle of the chute could be altered to distribute the
coal more evenly, whilst the sprinkler system was
intended to lay the often considerable clouds of dust
generated from certain types of fuel.

Ron ran over the controls for my benefit, and then
went on to give me a few tips. 'Always turn the water on
first. It may take a little time, but it makes a heck of
a difference if you want to keep yourself and the engine
clean. Now, before you touch the lever make sure that
there is nobody around and that the engine is correctly
positioned. Next, make sure that you know which way you
want the chute and that you are already pulling hard in
that direction before you release the catch. Sometimes
a large lump of coal will be lying on the chute and the
weight of this will pull the lever out of your hands,
causing it to drop the opposite way to what you intend.
You won't gain any laurels for putting half a ton of coal
on the cab roof, believe me! Always switch off a bit on
the light side. For one thing, a certain amount of coal
still drops even when the motor has stopped, and for
another you can always put a bit more on. So don't over-
coal any engine. It's a danger to everyone, yourself
included, and all spillage only has to be picked up again
by some poor blighter. However, you will sometimes be
asked to coal to maximum capacity, but this is a special
technique and I'll show you how when the time comes.'

I never thought that there was so much to be learned
about coaling engines, but taking this afternoon's
activities as typical, I realised that I was going to
get plenty of practise in during the next few months.
'I'll move her down a bit now,' said Ron, popping his
head round the corner of the hut to confirm that the
preceding engine was clear. 'Drop the chute so that it
points towards the rear of the tender first. Doing it
that way prevents coal from shooting out all over the
footplate; when it's filled up a bit I'll draw down,
and then you can tip it the other way so that it tops up
the front part without making a mess.' We proceeded as
planned and I once more realised that there is nothing
so effective as a practical demonstration for making a
lesson sink in and, although it was some considerable
while before I was accomplished in this art, I always
took a great delight in doing a neat and tidy job under
the coaling plant.

Down on the ashpit, Ron gave me further instructions.
'This is almost rough enough to warrant taking up the
firebars,' he said, nodding towards the great heap of
clinker and ash covering the grate, 'but I think we'll
ladle it out on this occasion. Get me a long and a
short shovel, a rake and a bent dart and we'll make a
start.' I jumped down on to the mounds of clinker,
which were piled on both sides of the track, and began
looking for the required implements. There was a short
shovel lying a few feet away and I pounced on it
eagerly. Almost immediately, heat struck through my
leather gloves, causing me to release my grasp.
'Crikey,' I thought, 'what a good job I was wearing
them.' Lesson one: never pick up a fireiron from the
ashpit without first spitting on it to see if it is hot.
I dragged it respectfully to a nearby standpipe and
cooled it down with a jet of water before handing it to
Ron. 'I see you're learning,' he said with a grin. I
obtained the other irons without any more trouble than
a singed right boot and joined my mate on the footplate.
'Sit up on the driver's seat out of the way and watch
for a while,' he puffed, for the sweat was already
trickling down his face.

I noticed that he had removed the deflector plate
and had placed this behind the hand brake column, so as
to give more room for manoeuvre through the firehole.
I also noticed that he was tackling the cleaning in the
well-tried manner of pushing live fire to the front of
the box and clearing the rear half first. 'It's

generally the best way,' he commented, after I had
brought this to his attention. 'Unless, of course, it's
so choked under the arch that you've got no room, in
which case it usually pays to pull four bars up and push
it out through the ash pan.' After breaking up the
clinker under the doors and pushing it forward, he
turned to me with a wave of his hand, indicating that we
were to change places. 'Right,' he gasped, mopping his
brow with a handkerchief. 'Ladle that lot over the side
with the short shovel.' I set to work with gusto, but
after a few minutes the shovel grew rapidly heavier and
hotter, and I grew heavier and hotter with it. My movements became slower and more laboured, and streams of
perspiration gushed from every pore. The muscles in my
arms and shoulders began to ache so that I could barely
retain a grip on that ton weight of a shovel.
Determined not to give in, I struggled on, staggering in
a daze of agony and gritting my teeth so as not to shout
out. Blinded by sweat and gasping for breath, I was
nearing the end of my tether when Ron laid a kindly hand
on my shoulder. 'That's enough, old fellow, let me have
a go now.'
    I fancy he had been testing me to see how far I would
go before giving in, but my obvious distress had been
too much for his sensitive nature and had thus put a
stop to my self-inflicted torture. However, my efforts
had at least cleared the rear half of the grate, so that
he was now able to give a really first-class demonstration of how to clean the front out. Using the long
shovel, Ron performed with a skill and swiftness that
made my eyes bulge. Knowing exactly what to do, he
wasted not one movement and, although he puffed and
sweated in the intense heat, he showed no sign of the
fatigue that I had been stricken with. I concluded that
experience and practise notwithstanding, you also needed
a lot of brute strength and stamina, and the sooner I
got down to some serious exercise to improve my physique,
the better. With the last shovel of clinker thrown over
the side, Ron pushed the fireirons clear of the cab and
slapped the dust from his overalls with his leather
gloves. 'Drop two or three shovels of coal under the
door now, but don't put too much on or you'll get choked
when you come to do the smokebox.' I did as requested
and shut the firedoors, remembering that you should
never move an engine after the fire has been dropped
without first doing this, otherwise cold air will be
drawn in and cause severe contraction stresses to be set

up in the firebox and tube plates, etc.

'If you've got your breath back now,' he said with an impish smile, 'we'll do the ash pan. Get down and stop me so that the damper door is just in front of one of the slaking pipes. The wind's blowing the wrong way down the pit, so you'll get covered in dust if you don't soak it well.' This accomplished, I slithered into the pit and, crouching well down, made my way towards the pan. These pits were brick-lined structures about four feet wide and three feet deep. The floor was cambered like a road and a water drainage gutter ran down either side. Midway along the pit and set in the floor was a metal grid, which allowed ash to fall through into a hopper below and when full, this hopper could be raised to tip its contents into a wagon set aside for the purpose. On either side of the grid were two sets of slaking pipes fixed to the pit side walls. These took the form of three-foot long L-shaped half-inch copper pipes, flattened at the outlet end to give a fan-shaped jet, and attached to a universal ball joint at the other. When in good working order, a very effective stream of water could be directed into the ash pan and, if one cared to take sufficient time, all the ash therein could be converted to a wet sludge.

As a cleaner I never relished going under an engine, but familiarity eventually banished my fears and now I rather enjoyed it. However, I did not relish raking out ash pans, particularly if the wind was in the wrong direction or the slaking pipes inoperative. The odd spot of hot oil or water dropping down one's neck was not too bothersome, but it could be very wet when the universal pipe joints leaked and when ash blocked the drainage channels, causing small lakes to form around one's feet. It was so on this occasion and, as I directed the main jet of water over the damper door, a fine curtain of spray drifted towards me from the general direction of the control valve. As it happened, I quite welcomed the cooling droplets on my overheated brow, and my overalls were in any case already soaked with perspiration. The pan was full to the bars with ash and by the time this had been cleared to my satisfaction I had an aching back to go along with my aching arms.

Emerging from the pit I saw that Ron was standing on the front framing holding a heavy spanner in his hand. 'I was waiting for you to finish before showing you this tip,' he called as I stood wiping sweat and dust

from my face with a decidedly soggy handkerchief.
'Slacken all the nuts first, and then tap the lugs off
except for the one furthest away from the hinge. Do
that last, and then when the smokebox door swings open
it won't knock you off the framing.' So saying, he
sharply smote the aforesaid lug, upon which the door
swung back allowing a small avalanche of char to pour
out, swirling onto the framing. 'Dig it out with the
firing shovel and throw it well clear downwind, like
this,' and Ron dextrously threw half a dozen shovels of
the black, unpleasant substance onto a large heap some
two yards from the smokebox. 'Come on up and have a go
then,' he said, dangling the shovel before me. I clambered up the front steps on to the framing and waded in.
The first shovel of char was a well-heaped one but as I
withdrew it from the smokebox, a goodish portion fell
from the blade, only to be whipped up in the airstream
created by the blower. I seemed to be suddenly engulfed
in a hot, gritty blizzard which got into my ears, nose
and eyes, and penetrated every crevice of my clothing.
I quickly realised that, unless I wanted to be smothered
in the stuff, I would have to go very gently indeed and
not get too much on the shovel. I suppose that cleaning
out a smokebox required far less effort than cleaning
either the fire or the ash pan, but I never did like the
job, mainly because I could do nothing to lay the dust,
and I also found the noise from the blower jet at close
proximity physically painful.

Ron was watching my performance from a safe distance
with some amusement, but he didn't say anything until I
had finished. 'Now wipe the joint faces clean of char
and close the door,' he instructed, adding as an afterthought, 'only fasten the two outer lugs.' I wrestled
with the heavy smokebox door and nearly fell off the
framing in the process. Why in God's name was everything so heavy on a locomotive, I thought, as I finally
managed to secure the lugs. Even the spanner was over a
foot long and weighed pounds! I rejoined Ron on the
footplate and tucked a few more shovels of coal under
the door as he prepared to move forward over the points
that led into Number Two shed. It was very necessary to
keep one's eyes open when moving about the yard.
Everyone seemed to be in such a rush and minor collisions were not at all uncommon even between experienced
crews. We proceeded slowly towards the shed, each in
our correct roles - Ron driving and myself walking in
front, pulling over the appropriate points. The arrival

and departure roads merged just outside the shed
entrance, so great care had to be exercised at this
point and it was always sound, and indeed official
policy, for the fireman to walk in first in order to
ascertain that no other engine was about to emerge and
that the table was secured in the correct position. On
more than one occasion an engine, possibly low on steam,
has passed from the bright sunshine outside into the
dark gloom of the shed without stopping, only to find
that the table was set for another road. Eighty tons of
metal down a six-foot hole causes quite a nuisance for a
while. . . .

I found a Class 2P at the far end of the arrival road
and, since the crew were disembarking, enquired if they
were leaving her there. 'I'm afraid the sheds are full
at the moment,' said the driver. 'We've been told to
park it here, so you'll have to do the same.' I later
discovered that this was a fairly common occurrence at
busy periods, and this is why two sets of marshalling
men were always on duty. Ron nodded when I advised him
of the situation, and he gently brought our engine to
rest against the buffers of the 2P. We topped up the
boiler, dropped some large lumps of coal in the back
corners of the grate, shut the firedoors and left the
damper open one nick. I collected our tool kit of four
spanners and dropped them into the bucket along with the
canister of detonators; then, with bucket and shovel
grasped firmly in one hand, slithered to the ground.
We normally left the two headlamps, the gauge lamp and
the coal pick on the engine, but were obliged to return
the rest of the tools to the stores, which was fortunately only a few yards away tucked into a corner of
Number Two shed. Having done this, I suddenly realised
that I felt as though I had been stranded in the desert
without water for a couple of weeks. My mouth and my
throat were so dry I could hardly talk. Ron must have
felt the same, because on entering the mess room we
both dived for the taps over that old sink. Never had
cold water tasted so good.

No sooner had we sprawled out on the bench and made
ourselves as comfortable as our still-steaming bodies
would permit than who should appear but Frank, the
foreman's assistant. He was in even more of a bustle
than usual and, after a quick glance around the cabin,
spotted us and came straight over. 'Sorry to give you
another one so quickly, Ron,' he said with genuine
concern, 'but we're on the block outside and the

2.00 p.m. men have gone.' He referred, of course, to
the 2.00 p.m. quota men who, with plenty of engines to
go at, had after three hours either finished or were
finishing their requisite six. 'O.K.,' sighed Ron, in a
manner which would have been appropriate to a French
aristocrat when mounting the steps to the guillotine.
'8608,' continued Frank, 'on the back road. She
shouldn't be a bad cop.'

Ron prudently filled the tea can with cold water
before we set out once more to find our engine. Our
Class 8F was the leading engine of three standing on the
rear road. We clambered aboard and went through the
usual check drill. A glance in the fire confirmed
Frank's assumption that she was not a bad cop. The
boiler was full, the pressure was showing 220, and the
tank indicated 3,000 gallons. 'I'm glad we've got an
8F,' said Ron as he wound her into forward gear. 'I'll
be able to show you how to clean a fire by getting the
bars up.' 'Do you always get the bars up on these then?'
I asked, out of genuine interest. 'Yes. 8s, 5s, 5Xs
and 'Crabs' are best tackled by pushing it out through
the ash pan. 'Crabs' are the worst, though. They only
have two sets of bars and they weigh a ton each.
Because they are so difficult to get out, some men
prefer to use a paddle, but I think that's even harder,
and in any case there's no need to get underneath to
rake out the front pan when you've already done it from
the top.'

We drifted gently down to the hopper and, as before,
obtained our coal from the goods end. Ron pointed out
that it was even more important to start with the chute
facing the rear of the tender on engines fitted with
tender doors, since large lumps of coal travelling at
high velocity could burst open the door catches and it
was very easy for this to happen unnoticed. Sometime
ago, he himself had managed to deposit a ton of coal on
the footplate in this manner. With the coaling completed
we were then able to move right down the pit so that our
front ash pan was over the grid. 'Right,' said Ron when
in position, 'All I want is the firebar tongs, and an
ash pan rake.' Once more I set off to search around the
piles of clinker and was fortunate to find the required
tongs quite nearby. They must have weighed nearly a
hundredweight, and with handles six feet long it was as
much as I could do to even carry them. With some effort
I propped the tongs against the engine steps and then
jumped down into the waterlogged pit in order to retrieve

the ash pan rake. Again, these rakes were all steel and, being fifteen feet long, were awkward things to carry around. By the time I arrived back on the footplate, Ron had laid bare the middle six firebars of the centre section with the aid of the engine's own short clinker shovel. 'Make sure that you pull some live fire into the back corners first,' he said as he noticed me peering into the firebox. 'You'll need it there if you want to save some.' Ron returned the clinker shovel to the fireiron compartment on the tender, and then with a mighty heave pulled the tongs on board. 'Give me plenty of room with these things,' he grunted as he wrestled the heavy implement through the firehole. 'The idea is to remove about four firebars from the middle of the grate - like this.' He clamped the jaws on the rear end of one of the selected firebars, and by grasping a massive handle in each hand he squeezed both inwards and downwards. At first nothing happened, so Ron bounced his whole weight on the handles so that the tongs became a sort of seesaw with the mouthpiece ring acting as the fulcrum. Suddenly the end of the bar jerked upwards and Ron was able to drag it backwards over the slope of fire and clinker so that it was lying just against the mouthpiece ring. 'Now this is the tricky part,' he grunted. 'If you are going to lose a bar in the ash pan, this is when it happens.' 'What are you going to do now then?' I said, wondering what form his next gymnastic exercise would take. 'I'm going to turn the bar over on its back and draw it out of the fire- hole,' and so saying, he wound himself round the tongs and then performed a sudden sideways half somersault; the bar clattered onto the footplate. 'The next one should be easier,' he gasped, ramming the fearsome instrument back through the firehole again. 'I should hope so,' I retorted, retrieving my cap from the foot- boards and retiring to the furthest corner. I must admit the last three firebars to be extracted did not require quite as much effort, but even so, by no stretch of the imagination could they be called easy. In due course I was to try my hand at this king-size dentistry and eventually became quite expert, but not before dropping a few hundred bars into ash pans and down hopper chutes, removing a square yard or two of skin from my knuckles and straining just about every muscle in my body.

The gap left by the four extracted firebars enabled entry to be gained to the front compartment of the

ash pan. This front compartment extended in an upward
slope to the rear of the second set of bars, while a
similar but smaller compartment served the third set of
bars. As Ron explained, we now had to clear the ash pan
before starting on the fire and this was accomplished by
inserting the long rake through the gap, and ramming
hard in the general direction of the front damper which
was, of course, fully open. Unfortunately, one of the
ash pan stays ran right across the line of fire, so to
speak, so the rake had to be manoeuvred over or under
this thoughtlessly placed obstruction. When properly
cleared, daylight could be seen shining faintly through
the open damper and work could then be started on
dropping the mixture of fire, ash and clinker into the
pan. It was advisable to drop only a small quantity at
a time, so that this might be easily cleared from the
ash pan. A larger amount tended to compact and this
then became very difficult to dislodge.

We took it in turns and I found that, although I was
soon a bath of perspiration again, it was not quite so
tiring as working with a clinker shovel. This was
mainly due to the fact that the weight of the rake rested
on the mouthpiece ring, and only pulling or pushing
movements were required. Having cleared the front two
sets of bars, live fire had to be pushed forwards from
the back corners and under the firedoors, so that it lay
on either side of the gap. Care had to be taken here,
since it was quite easy to inadvertently lose the fire
in the ash pan as well. A short clinker shovel was best
suited to this purpose, while a short slightly curved
engine rake was used to lift the clinker still lodged in
the rear of the grate. When Ron had dextrously pulled
the remaining live fire back under the door, I placed a
few shovels of fresh coal on it and closed the front
damper. 'Right,' said Ron, 'you go and clean out the
smokebox and I'll clear the rear ash pan.' I found that
he was able to do this with the curved engine rake while
standing at the side of the track below the cab. Meanwhile, I made my way on to the front framing armed with
the firing shovel. The smokebox door of a Stanier
engine was secured by a dart which fitted into an
elongated slot in a bar running across and inside the
front of the smokebox. The dart was attached to a hefty
handle which, when turned through 90 degrees, aligned
the dart with the slot and so enabled the door to be
opened. A similar handle attached to a lock-nut secured
the whole assembly and, when in the closed position,

allowed the door to be pulled very tightly on to its
seating. It was a very much more convenient design than
the circumferential lugs found on the old Midland
engines, and only a sharp tap on the locking handle with
the back of the shovel, followed by a few brisk turns,
was required to gain access. Pulling the door open was
less of a hazard than on a Class 4, since the framing
area was much more generous, but the size of the box on
first acquaintance was quite staggering. I found that
it was very hot indeed. The locomotive being so much
longer than a 4F, I had to get my head and shoulders
inside in order to reach the tube plate, even though I
was using a long-handled firing shovel. However, in ten
minutes the task was completed and, feeling somewhat
overcooked, I rejoined Ron. 'We've got to put her in
Number Three shed,' he said as we ran down the pit
towards the dead end.

Contrary to regulations, I jumped off the still-
moving engine as we passed over the points. This rather
dangerous manoeuvre, together with jumping onto moving
engines and riding on the tender or loco steps, was
widely practiced, mainly because it saved a lot of time
and effort. Surprisingly few accidents resulted from
these capers, which is probably why they were allowed to
continue, but occasionally someone managed to sober the
rest by putting his foot under a wheel. I recall being
witness to such a drastic piece of surgery when a young
fireman had three toes amputated on the spot.

Number Three shed was the only one with a sixty-foot
turntable and the only one capable of turning and
housing the larger engines. It was also the only one
without a roof. Having been bombed during the war, no
one had got around to replacing it, but the majority of
enginemen preferred it that way since the absence of
trapped smoke made conditions far more pleasant to work
in - except during torrential rain and the odd blizzard.
However, the absence of a roof apparently upset the
draughting arrangements of the adjoining and reconstruc-
ted Number One shed. A modern concrete structure had
been built to replace the original so effectively
removed by the Luftwaffe but whatever the cause, it was
an undeniable fact that smoke generally hung in an
asphyxiating layer down to about footplate level in this
shed.

Skipping lightly from the rear tender steps, I
galloped ahead into Number Three shed and ascertained
that all was clear before calling Ron in. He stopped

Leicester M.P.D., typical 'modernised' M.P.D. on the ex-L.M.S. Arrival
road passes under coaling plant and then continues as disposal pit,
23 April 1959. Below: Garratt 47998, one of the two Garratts which
retained their fixed bunkers standing on a departure road at Saltley
M.P.D. Waiting to return north to Toton after servicing on the shed,
30 January 1955.

Putting the bag in. A regular chore to be undertaken anywhere at anytime. Precise alignment was necessary, and crews had to learn the exact stopping point at every water column used. The slender pipe in the foreground is not part of the column, but the chimney of its attendant frost fire.

Coal spillage on the footplate gave rise to dirty, uncomfortable and even dangerous conditions. However, a few moments with brush and slaking pipe soon restored that 'scrubbed deck' look. Below: Turning upwards of one hundred tons of locomotive by hand could be hard work. Fortunately, modern turntables were also equipped with vacuum tractor motors powered by the locomotives' ejectors.

A typical rocking grate with the forward section in the open position.
These grates made light work of tedious fire cleaning. Below: Where no
tender doors were fitted, getting coal forward whilst running was hard
and dangerous work. This shows a Deeley Compound's tender with carefully
stacked coal at the point where it was most needed.

Raking out the ash pan was generally considered the dirtiest task during disposal operations. Some of the inevitable dust clouds could be laid by liberal use of the slaking pipe seen projecting from the righthand wall of the pit.

Arrangement board at Camden Town M.P.D. This is fairly typical of such boards to be found throughout the L.M.S. system at that period; 1 September 1936. Below: Although there was room to fire from either side in the roomy Stanier cabs as depicted by this crew on an 8F, it was more convenient for the fireman to work from the right as shown.

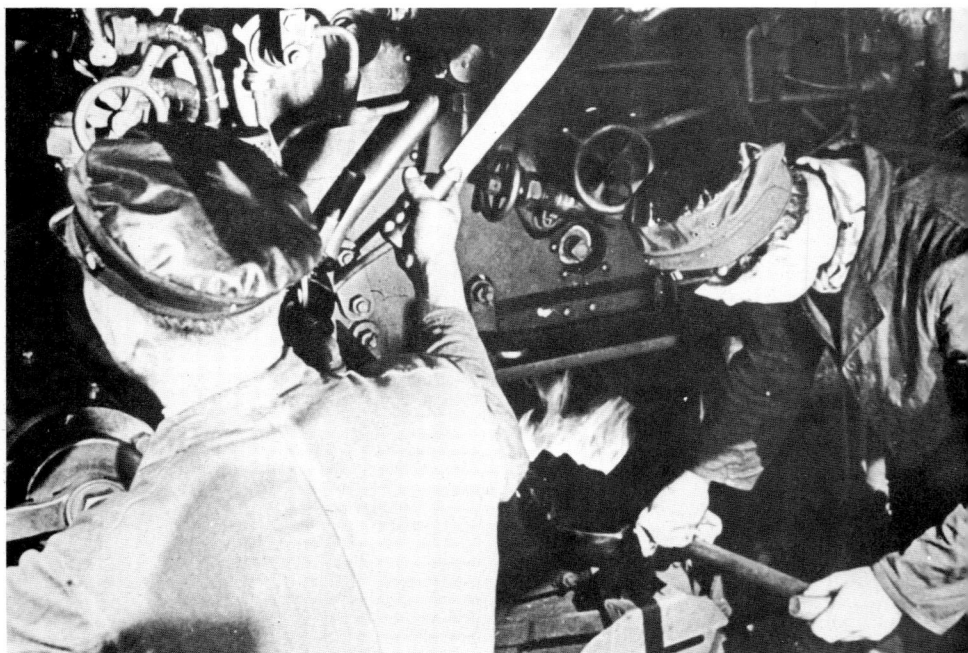

Showing what a fireman should not do, coal spillage on the footboards
forcing him to stand far to the left posterior-wise against the driver,
whilst the anti-glare shield obstructs his swing. Below: On joining an
engine, a fireman's prime task was to build up the firebed. In the
interests of safety and cleanliness it was policy to use the inevitable
spillage on the footplate first.

There were times when a driver could enjoy the luxury of being seated
in this stance. But often he would travel for miles with his head
thrust out in the slipstream, and with a rough riding engine he would
be obliged to stand whilst in motion.

nicely on the centre of the table and, since we only had
to turn as far as the second pit, I cranked it round by
hand. A preparation crew were good enough to relieve us
of the tool kit and, once again feeling very hot and
thirsty, we returned to the cabin. 'I think we'll have
a spot of supper now while we've got the chance,' said
Ron when we had removed the sweat and grime with revit-
alising cold water. Over our sandwiches we discussed
all manner of problems which might arise during disposal
and by the time we had washed the last crumbs down with
generous quantities of tea, I felt that at least I now
knew how to tackle most types of locomotives likely to
come on to the shed.

We were shortly given our next engine, a Fowler 2-6-4
tank. Ron groaned. 'They're a bit of a pig. Quite a
big firebox and no room to manoeuvre the fireirons.' I
had not been on one of these before and was interested
to see what they were like. Climbing into the cab, I
could appreciate what Ron meant. On other engines there
is a convenient space between the cab and tender so that
one can swing the handles of the fireirons practically
without restriction, but on a tank engine this gap is
closed by the rear of the cab. Due to their limited
water-carrying capacity, tank engines normally require
watering on arrival at the shed, and ours was no exception. As we pulled up under the passenger end of the
hopper, Ron told me to open the rear cab windows, since
this prevented the possibility of breakage by any small
pieces of coal that may penetrate between the bars of
the protective grilles. He also instructed me to tilt
the chute towards the cab since the bunkers on tank
engines are too short to allow the other method without
excessive spillage, and in any case the passage to the
shovelling plate was too tortuous for much coal to fall
onto the footboards.

Down on the pit Ron explained that again two methods
of fire cleaning could be adopted. Four firebars from
the front set could be removed and the fire dropped
through in the same manner as a 'Crab' (which they
resembled), only on this occasion the fireman had to get
underneath to clear the pan since a long rake could not
be used in the confines of the cab. Alternatively the
fire could be paddled out, using first a short and then
a long clinker shovel for the purpose. It was more
laborious, of course, than on a tender engine because
the shovel required skilled and delicate manoeuvring
round all the built-in obstructions. However, in this

instance Ron decided on the latter method since there
did not appear to be much clinker in the firebox.

We started off in the usual manner of initially
clearing the rear half of the grate and Ron allotted me
the first shift. I was immediately conscious of it
being much hotter on a tank engine, and was in trouble
straight away when I withdrew the first shovel of
clinker. The ring which forms the end of the handle
became hooked over the hand brake, and by the time I had
got this clear again I had deposited the contents of the
blade on the footboards. A nice little conflagration
started up as the red hot clinker and coal mixture made
contact with well-worn oil-soaked woodwork. Ron came to
the rescue with an accurately aimed bucket of water, and
amid clouds of steam and dust I started again. Gradually I noted the disposition of all the pitfalls, but
even so I found it much harder going than with a 4F.
Long before the back half was cleared I was tottering, so
Ron took over for a while. Working in turns, we ladled
out a surprising quantity of ash and clinker, for the
grate area on these 4P tanks was very deceptive. Caked
with dust, and soaked from the combined effect of spray
and perspiration, I crawled out to find that Ron was up
on the front framing attending to the smokebox. 'What a
grand fellow he's turning out to be,' I thought as I
asked him if I should take over. 'No thanks, I've
nearly finished now,' was the cheery reply, 'but you can
go and set the road for Number One shed, though.' I did
as requested, although I first had to wait for a couple
of engines coming out on the departure road.

Number One shed was always somewhat more difficult to
enter, since one first had to travel through Number
Three shed. By the time Number One shed's table had
been secured, someone wanted to come out of Number Three
shed and preference was always given to engines leaving
a shed. Then, when this matter had been dealt with, one
could find that a similar situation had now developed in
Number One shed. Thus a fireman could become involved
in an awful lot of running to and fro between the sheds
before finally getting settled on a vacant pit. It was
so on this occasion, and it took a full ten minutes of
haring backwards and forwards before I eventually
managed to call Ron in. The turntable in Number One
shed was also the most sensitive of the three to
balance. A few inches either way meant the difference
between turning with reasonable effort and a desperate
struggle. The shorter the wheelbase the more difficult

it seemed to be to achieve this balance; however, Ron
managed it on the second attempt and we were able to
stable the engine on one of the short pits set at
90 degrees to the arrival road without too much difficulty.

The heat had now gone out of the day but not out of
our bodies, and as we made our way back to the stores
Ron mopped his streaming face for the umpteenth time and
said, 'Do you see what I mean about the big tanks now?'
I replied that I certainly did, but I was glad of the
experience and in any case he must admit that at least
we had seen some variety.

The 8.00 p.m. quota men were now setting about the
incoming engines with some purpose, and we waited in the
mess room for nearly an hour before being given our
final engine of the day. Frank came over to Ron with a
disarming smile. 'I've got an easy one for you to finish
with,' he announced. 'Blimey, you've left it a bit
late,' was Ron's comment. '3014 on the back road. Coal
it with best and drop it in Number Two shed,' continued
Frank. 'That suit you?' Ron's face brightened at this
news. 'Ah! well, that's different,' he said. Then,
turning to me, he explained that 3014 was a 'Doodle Bug',
an Ivatt Class 4MT 2-6-0, and that these were equipped
with rocker grates, hopper ash pans and self-cleaning
smokeboxes. I had never been on one of these rather
ungainly-looking engines, although of course I had seen
them both around the shed and out on the road. With
their high framing, exposed motion and angular enclosed
cabs, their design showed a transatlantic influence and,
although not pretty, they certainly had an appearance of
utilitarian efficiency. However, from the gossip that I
overheard in the mess room their crews were not over-
impressed, complaining of indifferent steaming and
draughty cabs. During the next half hour, though, I was
to become endeared to them for life.

The daylight was failing rapidly as we once more
walked over to our engine. I clambered up unfamiliar
steps to the footplate and found Ron already peering at
the tank gauge in semi-darkness. 'We had better top it
up,' he commented. Whilst waiting for the tank to fill,
Ron prudently lit the headlamps, since a surprisingly
high number of incidents occurred on the shed precinct
due to engines not carrying lights, and furthermore
these were mainly at dusk. The Ivatt tenders carried
their coal in high-sided bunkers which stood up proud
from the rest of the tank and which were rather more

narrow than most. Therefore extra care had to be taken
during coaling operations. When Ron opened the regulator to move under the hopper I was quite amazed at the
sudden surge of acceleration. I subsequently found out
that these engines were incredibly lively and the
regulator needed a very light hand indeed when moving
around the shed. This faculty was, of course, a great
asset in stopping passenger trains for which work they
were eminently suited and, when I ultimately came into
the passenger links, I thought them superb. On
mentioning this point to Ron, he agreed that he knew of
no engine quicker off the mark than a 'Doodle Bug'.
'Do you know how a rocker grate works?' he asked when we
had rolled down over the ashpit. 'Only vaguely,' I
replied. 'Well, it's very straightforward really, and
why all the more modern engines are not converted as a
matter of routine when they go on for shopping I'll
never know.'

Ron detached a three-foot long lever from its
retaining clips, which were located on the side of the
cab beneath the fireman's seat, and quickly climbed down
to the ground. Pulling out a safety pin and flicking up
the locking catch, he then placed the lever on the
spigot and heaved upwards. The flaps in the bottom of
the ash pan opened with a clank, disgorging its contents
directly over the grid. 'Don't ever forget to open the
hopper first,' he advised as we clambered to the footplate again, 'or you'll be in real trouble.' With a
short clinker shovel he pushed some live fire forwards
just beyond the halfway mark. He then pulled up the
limiting catches and, with the lever firmly in place on
the righthand spigot, vigorously rocked the grate
backwards and forwards. I glanced over his shoulder to
see what was happening and was just in time to glimpse
fire, ash, and clinker disappearing through the gaps in
the rear half of the grate. He then returned the lever
to the midway position and closed the catches. Pulling
some fire back under the doors was the work of but a few
seconds, and he was then able to repeat this rocking
operation on the front half of the firebox. Two minutes
later, with the entire grate as clean as a whistle, I
was shovelling fresh coal into the box while Ron was
down on the ground once more to slam shut the ash pan
flaps. 'That's all there is to it,' he said with a
grin. 'The smokebox is self-cleaning, so we don't have
to bother with that. All we do now is to put her in the
shed.' 'Good lord,' I said, still somewhat

flabbergasted, 'no wonder you wished that every engine
was a rocker.' From then on I too was a rocking grate
enthusiast, but unfortunately at that time only a few
engines were equipped with this wonderful labour-saving
device. Like Ron, I couldn't help thinking that the
initial installation costs would quickly have been
recovered by the vast saving in time.

It was now almost completely dark and the yard lights
had been switched on. These were not the tall batteries
of brilliant lamps similar to those found in football
grounds and which we later became familiar with, but an
odd assortment dotted around at strategic points.
Rather like some street lamps, they tended to throw
pools of bright light with intervals of sharply contrast-
ing blackness in between. Running about the yard in
front of my engine, I found that I was jumping over
shadows and tripping over unseen obstructions, so I was
somewhat battered and confused by the time we arrived in
Number Two shed. Having parked on a vacant pit, I
decided to top up the boiler and it was then that I
discovered how efficient the injectors on these 'Doodle
Bugs' were. One could actually see the level in the
gauge glass rising, and it did not require much imagination to guess that these would have to be used in only
short bursts when out on the road. We were still on the
footplate when another set of shed men clambered aboard.
'Leave everything where it is,' said the driver. 'We've
got to prepare her for the Evesham.' 'Suits me,'
replied Ron, and so saying, grasped me by the arm and
guided me rapidly in the direction of the mess room.

A quick swill removed the surface traces of our day's
toil and, after collecting our lunch bags, we walked
round to the lobby to book off. It was still only
9.50 p.m. when I collected my cycle from the rack.
Enviously I watched Ron kick his motorbike into life and
after a cheery wave roar off up Duddeston Mill Road. I
followed at a very much more leisurely pace, a peculiar
stiffness seeming to have afflicted a great many muscles
which up to then I did not realise that I possessed. My
home was nearly three miles (mostly uphill) from the
shed, but this gave me time to reflect on the many events
of the day. I was booked with a first-class mate, and I
had the happy feeling that with his help and guidance I
was going to get an excellent grounding for the better
life to come.

I was not quite so early the following day and I still
felt rather tender and stiff. However, this soon wore

off as we tackled our first engine, a Class 3F which was
required in Number One shed for a washout. Engines had
the sludge washed out of their boilers at set intervals,
and when disposing of those booked for this operation
one had to be rather more fastidious than usual. The
fire naturally had to be dropped completely and, while
the engine was cold, any repair work which could not be
executed when in steam was carried out. The fitters,
not unreasonably, objected to any deposits of char, ash
or clinker left in the smokebox, ash pan or firebox
respectively. These objections, of course, came back to
us via the shed foreman, and it was no advantage to
incur his wrath for this or any other reason.

The day followed roughly the same pattern as the
preceding one except that we had different engines, and
the weather was hotter than ever. A Black Five came
after the 3F, and the method used on this was exactly
the same as with the 8F since they were practically
identical except for their wheel arrangements. Ron
raised my spirits considerably by telling me that Black
Fives of the 4700 and 4600 series were also fitted with
rocking grates, but alas none came our way that day.
Another 8F which gave the impression that it hadn't been
attended to for the better part of a year followed. It
caused Ron and I more hard work than any two previous
engines, for the entire grate was covered by a layer of
hard tenacious clinker, every inch of which had to be
literally chipped off. Luckily we were able to obtain
a Western dart to use for this task, otherwise we would
have been there all night. This formidable twelve-foot
long chisel was the only fireiron on the shed capable of
doing the job, and glory be to the gentleman who had the
foresight to borrow it from the other Region. Apart
from the clinker, the firebox was knee-deep in ash with
precious little fire left on top of it and, despite
Ron's skill, we were not able to save sufficient to
light up from. So long did we take with this engine
that both steam and water levels dropped very low and,
while I was digging my way through the solid bed of char
which was nearly level with the top of the blast pipe,
Ron negotiated with a colleague on the engine behind to
secure a tow into Number Three shed.

Eventually the task was completed, and the yard
foreman, who knew full well that he had given us a very
rough cop, tried to make amends next by presenting us
with a Class 3F 0-6-0 tank. Although a dreaded tank
engine, this 'Jinty' was so diminutive by comparison

that it turned out to be a piece of cake, as the saying
goes. The whole of the grate area was within easy reach
of a short clinker shovel, while there was so little
char in the tiny smokebox that a dust pan and brush
would almost have been quite adequate. We ended the day
with a Class 2P 4-4-0 which, having been used only
lightly with best grade coal, also proved to be
quite easy. And so the week progressed; it was hot and
dirty work, but we had a great variety of engines to deal
with and by Saturday night, I felt that I could now
tackle with confidence just about everything that might
come to the shed. However, knowing how, and actually
doing a job are poles apart, for I still did not possess
the necessary strength or stamina to dispose of the
average engine without a rest, by myself. This no doubt
would come in time, for after only one week my muscles
had taken on a much harder feel and I was sure that my
biceps had grown another half-inch.

The following week we were booked to arrive at
5.00 a.m. for preparation duties. Ron overtook me just
before reaching the depot and was already in the lobby
signing on when I walked in. 'Morning, mate, are you
fighting fit?' he enquired, obviously in the best of
spirits himself. I answered in the affirmative, and
after collecting my card from the clerk, joined him at
one of the several high writing tables which surrounded
the lobby. 'That's what we've got to get through today,'
he said, passing over a metal-backed wallet containing
the relevant job card. It listed six engines and the
jobs they were destined for, but very little other
information. 'Come on round to the engine board and I'll
show you how it works,' he continued, noticing my puzzled
expression. The board was located on the wall of Number
Two shed and was unique in that it was the centre of the
only well-lit area in the whole shed. In appearance it
was not unlike a huge black board and it listed all the
permanent jobs in chronological order. Beside these jobs
the foreman chalked the engine numbers allocated to them,
and whereabouts in the depot they were stabled, so that
provided one knew the job and its time, one could quickly
ascertain the engine and its location. Ron looked at his
job card and then at the board. 'Well, we've got the
first two anyhow,' he said, pointing out a couple of
engines with his finger. 'As with disposing, a lot of
chaps try to get through them as quickly as possible, the
driver taking one and the fireman another,' he went on,
'but it will be a while before you are ready for that.

To start with, it will be better to work together until
you get the hang of everything.' I nodded my consent.
'Is 4201 in Number One shed the first then?' I enquired.
'Yes,' said Ron. 'See if you can find her and I will
join you there when I've dropped my traps in the locker.'
    I made my way round the table and entered Number One
shed and as usual it was very gloomy, with a great cloud
of raw smoke hanging in a thick layer beneath the roof.
It was quite impossible to make out the smokebox numbers
of engines on the other side of the table pit, so I was
obliged to walk round twelve of the possible 23 berths
before spotting her. My first impression on gaining the
cab was that of utter dismay. Coal lay strewn all over
the footplate, and everything was coated in soot. She
had obviously been in for a washout and had spent the
last few days completely at the mercy of energetic
preparation crews who had effectively stripped from her
everything that was removable. Even one gauge glass
protector and the driver's pedestal were missing.
However, there was a good fire in the box, the boiler
was just about full and there was 140lbs. per sq.in.
showing on the pressure gauge. My first task now was
to draw the tools and lamps from the stores and I set
off hot-foot in that direction. On arrival, I gave the
engine number to the storeman, who merely shrugged
apologetically and said he could only furnish me with a
firing shovel and a seven-eighths spanner. I scurried
back to the engine bearing my trophies. Ron was just
climbing down from the footplate. 'In a bit of a state,
isn't she?' he murmured as I galloped up to him. 'They
haven't any tools in the stores,' I gasped somewhat
breathlessly. 'I'm afraid that's not unusual at this
time of a morning. You'll just have to scrounge around
the shed and rob another engine. The arrival road may
be your best bet.'
    Ron went on briefly to explain that in the good old
days locomotives had their own tools and each was
stamped with the engine number. However, when Josiah
Stamp instituted his economies in the 1930s, tools were
kept in a common store, booked out to an engine for its
turn of duty and then returned to the store when this
was completed. The idea, of course, was that a considerable reduction in the number of sets required could be
effected. Unfortunately, in the early 1950s, such was
the shortage of equipment that much time was wasted by
crews running around trying to find some. Very often
they were forced to wait for engines coming on to the

shed before they themselves could depart. Regrettably,
this deplorable state of affairs persisted for many
years, and it was not until the late 1950s that sufficient tools became generally available. The situation was
always at its worst during the early part of the day and
at its best in the late evening, when a glut of engines
seemed to arrive at the shed.

I looked desperately around Number One shed for
engines with lamps, but there were none to be seen.
Being slightly nearer to Number Three shed at the time, I
tried in there first, but again drew a blank. This is
damned silly, I thought, beginning to feel a trifle
ruffled, and dashed back across Number One shed into
Number Two where, wonder of wonders, I spied a 2P with a
lamp on its front bracket. I quickly gathered this up,
together with the gauge lamp, rear lamp and coal pick.
I was lucky. The engine had just been turned off, and no
doubt in another minute this lot would have been whisked
away by some other foraging preparation crew. Not daring
to put anything down, I walked over to the stores again
where I filled and trimmed the lamps.

Ron in the meantime had also been out on a hunting
expedition and had found an oil bottle, a feeder and a
gauge frame spanner. 'There's a decent slaking pipe on
that one there,' he said, pointing to a 3F standing two
pits away. I deposited my precious equipment on the
footplate and, picking up the seven-eighths spanner,
scampered over to the 3F, anxious in case anyone else
should get there first. The slaking pipe was secured by
a seven-eighths brass nut and a hefty heave with the
spanner sufficed to free it. Whilst still on the footplate, the thought suddenly struck me that fireirons
might be concealed behind the heap of coal on the tender
and a quick ascent into the smoke clouds revealed that
there was indeed a full set. I descended with my booty
as quickly as possible and, after pausing for a brief
coughing session, clattered back to our engine with the
fireirons in tow. By now I was soaked with perspiration
and I came to the firm conclusion that if anything,
preparation was even more energetic than disposal.
After depositing the fireirons on the back of the tender,
I attached the slaking pipe, and still with the seven-
eighths spanner in my hand clambered round the framing
to attend to the smokebox lugs. I pulled off the
sandbox covers on my way and made the not entirely
unexpected discovery that not one of them was more than
half full. We were just about as far from either of the

sand ovens as one could be at Saltley, so my heart
didn't exactly pound with joy, although it was very soon
pounding with exertion. First I had to find the
confounded buckets, which on this occasion were well
hidden in a dark corner behind the tender of a 2P in
Number Two shed. Then came the strenuous work of
hauling the sand across to the engine, which at two
buckets per sandbox meant six trips. After only the
second agonising journey my arms felt as though they
were being torn out of their sockets and I desperately
wished that I could find a wheelbarrow. After the
fourth trip, Ron declared that he had completed the
oiling and he would bring the engine on to the table,
since we were now falling behind schedule. He did this
by himself while I staggered back with more sand.

The final trip found me at the engine in such an
exhausted state that I had neither strength to lift the
buckets up on the framing nor sufficient breath to call
for help. Fortunately Ron, realising my predicament,
came to my aid. 'O.K., old son,' he said with a
partially concealed smile, 'secure the table in Number
Three shed and we'll get outside.' I nodded in answer,
being still short of breath, and just managed to fore-
stall another preparation crew who were ready to bring
out a Class 8F.

The points were correctly set for the departure road,
so as Ron trundled slowly over the turntable I hopped on
the engine steps, and then climbed slowly up to the
footplate. 'Getting a sweat on, mate?' said Ron with a
broad grin. 'It was those blasted sandboxes,' I replied
vehemently. 'Yes,' he said sympathetically, 'they can
be real rough work at times, particularly with a high
framed engine such as a Black Five. By the way, we've
got to drop her on the back departure road, so we'll top
up the tank at the water column there.'

While the tank was filling, I went across to the
arrival roads where a couple of engines were now
standing, and managed to collect the two spanners, the
bucket and the can of detonators, of which we were still
deficient. Meanwhile Ron set about the task of tidying
up the footplate. A lot of preparation crews never
bothered to do this but, as Ron said, while you were
filling up the boiler, it was no trouble to quickly
hose the dust off the footboards, and this made things
so much more pleasant for the men who were to work her.
We moved up to the end of the departure road, and after
screwing the hand brake hard on, dropping the damper,

closing the firedoors, setting the reversing screw in
mid-gear and opening the taps, we departed leaving her
reasonably spic and span.

Our next engine was a Class 8F in Number Three shed,
and as we walked over Ron suggested that we removed
everything from a Class 4F that had just arrived, since
it was unlikely that the stores had much to offer yet.
Everything, that is, except the firing shovel which was
a short-handled one, and the seven-eighths spanner which
the disposal men would require to open the smokebox door
with. We arrived at the 8F and found it in a much better
state than the previous engine. At least the cab wasn't
covered in smuts, the water tank was just about full and
there was a full complement of fireirons lodged in the
tender compartment. On the debit side, though, steam
pressure was a little low at 80lbs. per sq.in.; a good
stir round with the rake was called for. Unfortunately
there was insufficient fire under the doors to cover all
the grate and, realising that I would have to do this in
stages, I managed to spread what there was evenly over
the rear half. Opening the back damper, I left this to
burn up under the influence of the blower while I went
off in search of a firing shovel and seven-eighths
spanner. The stores were again able to supply a firing
shovel of the correct size, albeit a somewhat battered
specimen, but they were still short of spanners. However, while I was at the window filling the lamps, a
full set arrived and I was able to extract the one
required.

So far, things were not quite such a mad dash as with
the 4F, mainly because I had enjoyed better luck in
acquiring the tools. No extra time was allowed for
hunting around for equipment and, when the original study
had been conducted to fix how long it should take to
prepare the various classes of locomotives, it was
assumed that all tools could be drawn without delay from
the stores. Normally 45 minutes was scheduled for
engines rated 4F, 3P and under, while 4P Compounds and
engines rated above 5 MT were allowed one hour. This
was loosely based on the time it took to raise steam.
On the whole, men accepted the additional burden of tool
hunting with commendable indifference, since it was
largely in their own interests that the engines were
ready to book off the shed at the correct time. If they
had prepared their own engine, then any excessive delay
could well result in a cancellation of their job, and
they might be relegated to shed work. In the case of

preparation crews, the sooner they finished their
prescribed number of engines, the sooner they could go
home.

I arrived back at the 8F to find Ron still busy with
the oiling, and I noticed that no black smoke was
visible at the chimney. Looking into the firebox showed
that the fire I had spread around was now burning
brightly, so I covered this with a dozen shovels of coal
before climbing on to the framing to check the automatic
lubricators and those benighted sandboxes. One cannot
look directly into the sandbox of an 8F since, unlike a
4F, the box is filled via a cranked tube some six inches
in diameter. The technique we used to determine the quantity contained therein was simple. If one could see
sand at the bottom of the tube, then it was full enough.
If it was not visible, then one filled it until it was.
I breathed a very deep sigh of relief when I found that
all were full, as indeed were the lubricators, and I
mused on the irony of this engine being only a few paces
from the sand oven and yet not requiring any sand. Such
is life!

All effort could now be concentrated on raising steam
and, with this prime consideration in view, I once more
opened the firedoors to see how things were progressing.
The fresh coal was burning well, so it was now possible
to spread this to the front half of the grate, since
until that area was covered no results would be registered on the pressure gauge. I achieved this by using
the clinker shovel, experience having taught me that
this was a most effective tool in these circumstances.
By digging the blade into the fire under the door and
by using a sort of seesaw action I was able to deposit
pockets of bright fire all over the bare bars at the
front end. Then, by filling in the gaps with a thin
layer of well-chosen cobbles, it was only a matter of a
few minutes before the whole bed was thoroughly ablaze.
After that, by firing a small quantity of coal on to
the brighter areas, and with both the blower and the
front damper wide open, pressure soon began to build up.

'How's she looking now?' called Ron, who had just
completed his oiling. 'Beginning to move - in fact,
it's up to ninety,' I answered. 'Right, I'll just nip
over to the engine board and see what else is down for
us,' he replied, and turning on his heel vanished
through the entrance to Number One shed. I was still
tidying the footplate when a few minutes later Ron's
head suddenly appeared in the gap between tender and

cab. He craned his neck so as to see the pressure
gauge, which by now was climbing past the 150lbs. per
sq.in. mark. 'O.K., mate, bring her forward,' he
shouted. 'Me?' I replied, more than somewhat surprised.
'Yes, come on, I've got the table,' and with that, he
walked back to the control position and leaned on the
single retaining catch, waiting.

Things are looking up, I thought, for this was the
first time Ron had asked me to move an engine. I
quickly knocked over the steam brake handle, released
the tender brake, and wound her into full forward gear.
Leaving the taps open, I flicked across the small
ejector valve and, as the brakes came off, I gave a
short hoot on the whistle before easing open the regulator. Steam hissed noisily from the cylinder cocks and
she glided smoothly forwards. I gave another little
heave on the regulator before snapping it shut and then,
leaning out of the side window so as to judge my speed
more accurately, I listened for the tell-tale clunks as
the wheels passed over the gap between the pit and table.
Five clunks for the engine, and one, two, hand poised on
brake ready for the sudden application, three! I
knocked over the handle and we eased to a halt just
about in the correct position. Feeling mighty pleased
with myself, I once more applied the hand brake, for we
had to turn the engine through nearly 180 degrees and I
knew Ron would use the vacuum motor.

'Blow up!' he bellowed when the hoses were connected.
I wound open the brass wheel of the large ejector and we
started to rotate slowly so that the engine pointed west-
wards. This time we had to leave her on the departure
road next to the one where we had stabled the 4F, and
Ron kindly allowed me to drive while he ran in front
setting the points. Like many young drivers who until
quite recently had been firing, he realised that, apart
from being a necessary part of the training, allowing
the fireman to move the engine about the yard helped to
relieve the monotony of shed work. It also gave the
driver a chance to assess his mate's potential capabilities so that if, and when, he decided to tackle quota
work, he could do so with a higher degree of confidence.

After the 8F, we prepared a 3F and a Compound, which
Ron did not relish because of the difficulty and
additional work involved in oiling the inside motion.
We then allowed ourselves a short break for lunch, and I
must admit that I was grateful for a chance to sit down
for a while. Galloping around in search of tools and

fetching sand was having a peculiar effect on my legs.
All too soon this brief respite was over and we were
soon hard at it, preparing another 4F. This in turn was
followed by a Black Five and the day was finally rounded
off with a 'Crab'. As the afternoon wore on, so the
tool situation gradually improved, which in part compensated for my rapidly increasing fatigue, and I was
actually able to draw all the equipment I required for
the Five and the 'Crab' direct from the stores. We
eventually booked off with half an hour to spare and, as
I once more pedalled slowly home, I concluded that in
respect of the amount of energy expended, there was
nothing much to choose between disposal and preparation.
In the case of the former, it was the top half of the
body that took all the stress, whereas with the latter
the effort was biased towards the lower appendages.

This really set the pattern for the rest of the week.
The jobs were always the same, though of course the
engines were usually different, and after the first day
Ron allowed me to drive alternate engines, irrespective
of their class. When time permitted, he showed me how
and where to oil them, and how to set the motion so that
it was in the most convenient position. Also he pointed
out the most important parts to check and examine for
possible causes of failure and, whilst I found this side
of our work very interesting indeed, I soon discovered
that oiling can be far dirtier than anything a fireman is
supposed to do during preparation.

This particular week was somewhat outstanding in that
shed work was enlivened by a spate of collisions and
incidents of gradually increasing severity until at
lunchtime on Friday an accident occurred which could
well have resulted in tragic consequences. It all
started when a senior driver nudged the shed wall when
turning off a Class 5 in Number Three shed. He admitted
to an error of judgment and, apart from putting a slight
bulge in the aforesaid wall, which was the common one
shared by Number One and Number Three sheds, little harm
was done. However, this minor incident seemed to open
Pandora's box and release the jinx which reigned over
Saltley for five days. Not wishing to be left out of
things, one of the quota men effectively punched a hole
clean through the canalside wall of Number Three shed
with an 8F, and deposited two tons of assorted masonry
into a twelve-ton open wagon which was conveniently
parked on the track outside. The following day, some
marshalling men got carried away and a dead engine which

they were manoeuvring for the fitters decided to run off
on its own and constructed a neat third exit in Number
One shed. Getting thoroughly into the spirit of compet-
ition, a Passed Cleaner who had no business to be
driving at the time demolished, with the aid of a Class
8F, another section of poor old Number Three shed's wall
adjacent to the diesel oil storage tank.

Meanwhile the men out in the shed yard, intolerant of
being outdone by their colleagues inside, tore the side
out of a Class 5 tender which was standing foul on one
of the disposal pits. The day's destruction was rounded
off by a substantial head-on collision between a Black
Five, which had been prepared for the Carlisle and which
had been backed under the hopper to top up with coal,
and a 4P tank engine manned by an eager disposal crew
who failed to realise that the Five would be coming back
up the arrival road. It buckled the Black Five's front
framing and removed a buffer from the tank engine. This
campaign to deplete Saltley's locomotive stud was firmly
re-established on the Thursday when a Super D and a
Class 3F, which were coupled together for the convenience
of a disposal driver, ran away unmanned down to the stop
block at the end of the ashpits. They clouted this
formidable and ancient structure with sufficient violence
to cause extensive damage to both engines' buffer beams
and framings. For any two of these accidents to happen
in any given month would be unusual; for all to happen
within the space of less than a week was incredible.

Nothing more occurred until the climax of Friday
lunchtime. One of the quota men had disposed of a
Compound and, whilst waiting to enter Number Two shed,
had filled the boiler to a greater degree than was
strictly wise. This also had the effect of reducing the
steam pressure to little over 100lbs. per sq.in. Now
the steam brake on a Compound is notoriously ineffective,
particularly when pressure is low. The designers in
their wisdom envisaged their being used only on trains
fitted with a continuous braking system. Another
awkward thing about Compounds is that they often tend
not to respond to an initial opening of the regulator,
and there is a considerable delay before the wheels
start to rotate. Moreover, 24 turns of a very stiff
reversing screw from full forward gear to full backward
gear preclude any swift changes in direction, should the
need arise to help out on the lack of braking power.
All these factors can add up to a very lethal combination
when trying to manoeuvre hastily in confined places.

Familiarity breeds contempt, and when one has
executed an operation successfully many hundreds of
times it is easy to relax one's concentration for a
moment. Whatever the reasons, the Compound was given a
good handful of regulator when it seemed reluctant to
move off the table. Then she did move - with a rush,
the great seven-foot drivers slipping violently, and all
that momentum could not be arrested in the few yards
available by those feeble brakes. The result was inevitable. The Compound, still travelling at a fair speed,
jumped the pit stops and crashed tender-first with
terrific force into the shed wall which divided it from
the main office. So great was the impact that a section
of wall roughly the size of the tender exploded into the
office, and some portions of the thick brickwork flew
right across the room and through the windows opposite.
Only a few minutes earlier members of the office staff
were working in this area and, had they not just retired
for lunch, would certainly not have lived to see another
day. The damage took several days to repair and, being
right next to the enginemen's lobby, no member of the
footplate staff could fail to see the extent of the
devastation or realise the possible consequences.
Fortunately, it had a very sobering effect on all
concerned and seemed to exorcise our jinx for, although
incidents did occur from time to time in the future,
they were infrequent and isolated affairs, quite within
the bounds of reason for a motive power depot the size
of Saltley.

When Ron arrived for work on Saturday morning his
normally happy features wore a worried expression, for
his wife had been taken ill and was in hospital. He had
arranged to exchange turns with another driver in the
link, Doug Pinkerton, who was booked on a morning shift.
Doug Pinkerton, known as Pinky to all his acquaintances,
was a lean, powerfully built Brummie of just under six
feet in height. Not even his own mother would have
described him as handsome but his chunky, square-cut
features had a pleasant alert expression. He had that
peculiar gift of leaving a trail of destruction and
chaos behind him wherever he went, and everything he
touched seemed miraculously to fall apart. His talents,
however, extended to his having one of the most compre-
hensive route cards at Saltley, for he signed from
Bristol and Bath in the south-west to Carlisle in the
north, and during the many weeks I was to work with him
he proved to be a first-class engineman.

We first met in the enginemen's lobby at about 9.45
on the Monday evening and, after introducing ourselves,
he suggested that we went round to the cabin to mash
some tea before joining the shed bus in the car park.
Two Ford 26-seater utilities and one Bedford 12-seater
were stationed at Saltley for the purpose of conveying
engine crews to and from certain predetermined pick-up
points in the locality. As we doubled round to the
cabin (Doug, I duly found, did everything at the double)
he explained that he always liked a drink of tea before
starting work. 'What is the Bromford job then?' I
puffed as I trotted alongside in an effort to keep up
with him. 'Garratts,' he shouted, for Doug always spoke
loudly, rather like the first mate of a clipper ship
calling to his men to reef the top gallants. 'Garratts?'
I replied, nonplussed. 'Yes, Garratts. They are too
big to dispose of on the shed, so they coal them here
and then take them down to Bromford where we dispose and
prepare them before they work the empties back to Toton.
It can be quite cushy - sometimes you only get one all
night, but on other occasions you can get three or four
and then you really earn your keep.'
So that was it, then. Same sort of work but a different location. It made a change and I was very
interested to have a close look at a Garratt. These
monsters could be seen fairly frequently trundling
around the area with long strings of wagons in tow, but
so far I had never been on one. Originally 33 were
built with the prime intention of handling, with only a
crew of two men, what was really a double train. That
they could do this in practice was not entirely
surprising, since they were really a double engine -
like two 'Crabs' back to back, sharing a large common
boiler. The Garratt-powered 100-wagon, London-bound
coal trains are now past history; like many other over-
large creatures they could not adapt quickly to changing
conditions, so that when congestion increased during and
immediately after the war their long trains could not be
accommodated in the majority of lay-bys and sidings.
Thus, when their tremendous hauling capacity could not
be fully utilised, and their achilles heel of inadequate
axle bearings proved increasingly expensive, their days
were numbered. At that time, though, quite a number
found themselves on westbound coal trains from Toton and,
although most of them terminated at Birmingham, some did
get through to make the descent of Bromsgrove bank,
usually at a hair-raising speed.

The disposal area at Bromford consisted of two roads,
one with an ashpit, which converged into a single line
leading to a turntable and a dead end just beyond.
Between the two roads was a water column and almost
opposite this on the far side of the ashpit was a small
stoutly-built wooden hut. As we approached, I could see
the dim outline of a Garratt standing at the near end of
the pit road, looking more massive than ever in the dark.
'We'd better check her first,' said Doug, hauling a
rubber-cased torch out of his pocket. I followed him on
to the footplate and viewed the unfamiliar surroundings.
As the relieved driver had said, all was well, the
boiler was full, the pressure gauge was showing 160lbs.
per sq.in. and when Doug pulled open the firedoors a
healthy flicker of flame rolled up from the back corners.
I had not realised just how large the Garratt firebox
was, and I squatted for a moment peering round that vast
cavern in awe. Doug must have read my thoughts. 'Yes,
you can get a fair old bit of coal in there, my lad,' he
said with a chuckle. 'In fact, you can shovel a ton and
a half at one session and then not fill it.' I could
well believe that for, although the grate area was large
by any standards, it was the depth that was so impressive - no wonder that most of them were fitted with
rotating hoppers, which rolled the coal forwards at the
touch of a lever. 'Come on,' said Doug, 'she'll be all
right for hours. Let's get settled in the cabin. I've
my supper to get.'
We had just about finished our meal when a Garratt
arrived freshly coaled from the shed. It had rolled on
to the pit almost unnoticed while we were engrossed in
our chatting and eating. Thus feasted, we felt better
able to tackle the monster which had been patiently
waiting outside. Doug explained, to my relief, that
cleaning the fire on a Garratt was not too bad really,
since they were equipped with a section of grate which
dropped in the form of a flap, in the lefthand front
corner of the firebox. This enabled the fire to be
pushed straight through into the ash pan. Providing
that one man cleared the pan while the other pushed out
the fire it was fairly straightforward.
Everything about a Garratt was outsized. The tank,
for example, seemed to take ages to fill in absorbing
its 4,500 gallons of water, but Doug made good use of
this time by clearing the fire from the area above the
flap. When eventually the tank was filled, we drew
ahead across the table before dropping back on the pit

road. Doug managed in his boisterous way to make the
Garratt slip, and I noticed afterwards that eight
exhaust beats emerged from the chimney for every revolution of the wheels instead of the previous four. 'This
sometimes happens,' he explained when I questioned him
on the point. 'Being in effect two separate engines
they can come out of synchronisation, and then they
really do use up a lot of fuel.'

When in position over the pit, Doug told me to clear
the ash pan first, and when this was done he would start
to drop the fire. Having dampers at either end of the
pan meant that I could both push and pull the contents
out and there was no need for me to go underneath,
although it did entail working from first one side and
then the other. Although not particularly full of ash,
it took quite some time because the pan, in keeping with
all the rest of the engine, was so large. At last I was
ready and shouted to Doug. For what seemed hours
quantities of fire and clinker dropped into the ash pan,
and I strove with all my might to keep pace with it.
There was no chance of a rest, for to allow the clinker
to build up would have resulted in a jam - it just had
to be cleared as fast as it came through. This was as
bad as anything that I had yet tackled in disposal work,
worse really, since you could at least have a short rest
when on a normal engine, and I was soon soaked with
perspiration while my back and arms were numb with
fatigue. When just about on my last gasp, Doug threw
down the long rake which he had been using and called
out that all was finished. Never had I been so thankful
to hear those words, and by the time that I somewhat
painfully regained the footplate, Doug had repositioned
the flap and was filling a feeder from the oil bottle.
'Just fill up the back of the box,' he said with a grin,
'while I nip round with the oil can. Anything that will
go through the hole is small enough,' he continued,
indicating some huge lumps of coal lying on the shovelling plate, and with that he disappeared quickly down
the steps.

I started to shovel steadily away, manhandling large
lumps through the firehole in much the same manner as
one might load a heavy howitzer. After fifteen minutes
or so I was beginning to puff and blow more than
somewhat, and by then still only one torpedo-shaped
piece of coal was showing below the ring. When this
operation was accomplished we returned to the cabin once
more, and with no more activity imminent settled

comfortably on the benches. Soon we succumbed to the
soporific warmth of the stove that was burning and for
three hours we slumbered peacefully, until rudely awak-
ened by the arrival of some more Toton men who were
after the first Garratt. Still in a bit of a daze, we
moved the second engine forward over the table so as to
allow them access to the departure road. When they had
gone, I shovelled more coal into the rear of the firebox
and, this being done to our satisfaction, we returned
the Garratt to its original position. We had no more
visitors, so after a brief tidy round we walked slowly
towards the road bridge where our bus was due to collect
us just after 6.00 a.m. Despite my pleasant three-hour
snooze I still felt tired, but was able to enjoy the
ride home through the quiet sunlit streets, reflecting
that of all the shed jobs so far this seemed to be the
best.

The rest of the week at Bromford was as variable as
Doug had first indicated, with nights of what almost
amounted to indolence alternating with nights of intense
activity. Ron's wife had now entered hospital for a
further operation and he elected to work under the quota
system with me. I naturally complied, since the advantages of free evenings were only too apparent. The yard
foreman and his assistants were extremely sympathetic to
Ron's predicament and made every effort to allocate only
the easy cops to us. For example, every rocker grate
engine that came on the shed was somehow reserved
exclusively to ourselves. Nor did the other disposal
crews object; indeed, they went out of their way to
smooth our path and render every assistance possible,
which to my mind was a most generous display of comrade-
ship. Being constantly on the move it was, of course,
hard work, and I found myself entirely responsible for
one engine while Ron handled the other. He naturally
performed the examinations on all engines and wherever
possible we moved into the shed together, but working in
this manner served to provide the right sort of experience which promoted a great deal of self-confidence I
would not have acquired anything like so quickly in the
normal way. I also enjoyed the unquestionable benefits
of being back home again in time for tea. In fact, on
one memorable afternoon when I had received three
rockers in succession, I found myself in the unique
position of booking off exactly an hour and a half
after booking on.

It was on the Saturday of that week that Ron quietly

announced the doctors had confirmed that his wife was in fact suffering from an incurable cancer and they gave her at the most but a few months to live. After this sad news I only worked with Ron on one or two occasions when our turn of duty coincided with times convenient to his responsibilities at home, for he was obliged to exchange turns almost every week. I therefore found myself booked with a great variety of drivers, the advantage of which was that I got to know intimately a large number of them, which stood me in very good stead in the following years.

In October a vacancy occurred in the Bank Pilot link and, as senior fireman, I was promoted to fill it. Although I had enjoyed some extremely happy moments and learned quite a lot in the Washwood Heath link, I was very glad at last to once again go beyond the shed limits and get down to the real job of firing. It was, therefore, with some considerable excitement that I looked forward to joining my new mate, Bill Sturmy, at the very civilised hour of 8.00 a.m. on the following Monday morning.

V

THE BANK PILOTS

As previously described, the Bank Pilot link
consisted of six Class 3F 0-6-0 engines operated by
eighteen sets of men working three shifts of approximately eight hours duration. That they frequently
enjoyed more than eight hours was no fault of the
planners, who could not have possibly foreseen the
severe congestion prevalent in 1950. In their wisdom,
they had arranged for the pilots to come off the shed at
carefully spaced intervals so as to ensure that no two
crews would require relief at the same time, which meant
that five out of the six engines would always be
immediately available for duties. However, since the
drivers had their full share of human frailties, many of
them spent a great deal of time cultivating the friendship of appropriate signalmen in order to try and be at
some particular position on the bank when their relief
booked on. In other words, if the driver in question
desired overtime he would arrange, if at all possible,
to be as far from the shed as this four-mile stretch
would allow. If for some reason he wanted to book off
early, then relief right outside the loco was the ideal
to aim for. We firemen were, of course, innocent of
these machinations on first joining the link, but
having no other option quickly fell in with our mates'
inclinations. All the fretting, scheming and bickering
that occurred amongst the drivers did seem rather petty,
but it was generally treated with tolerant amusement.

Being in effect a small close-knit team performing a
rather special function tended to develop in the crews
a somewhat insular outlook and, because the job was as
near routine as any job could ever be on the railways,
a certain element of boredom inevitably crept in. The
drivers, having experienced just about every possible
contingency and knowing every sleeper of the track
intimately, could - and for that matter sometimes did -
execute their duties with their eyes closed. I found
myself introduced to this select little group when I
met Bill for the first time that Monday morning in late
October. He was a stockily-built individual of about
my own height, sporting an amply filled waistcoat and
an aggressive jaw. He wore a cloth cap in preference
to a uniform one, and initially seemed reluctant to

indulge in much conversation. However, after the formal
introductions were completed, he did unbend to the
extent of divulging the number of the engine we were to
relieve and that we had better find out where it was.
'We'll go and see the controller at Duddeston Mill box,'
he said gruffly after collecting some items from his
locker and then, as we walked sedately the few yards to
the signal box, he sniffed the air, glanced at the sky
in a professional manner and pronounced, 'Wind's in the
north-east. Hope they've got a sheet.' 'A sheet?' I
enquired. 'Yes, a sheet for the cab. Otherwise we'll
be starved all day, standing wrong way to the weather
with the wind in this direction.'

I had already discovered that it could be most
unpleasant and decidedly wet if raining, when running
tender-first or merely just standing, if the wind was
blowing directly into the back of the cab. Pilots were
always brought out facing up bank towards the west, and
because the job necessitated a lot of standing around
and in any case fifty per cent of the running was tender-
first, conditions in the cab could be rendered very
uncomfortable in the teeth of a stiff nor-easter.
Tarpaulins rigged between the tender and cab roof made a
great difference, since they not only kept the wind and
rain out but also kept the heat trapped inside and,
although inconvenient at times if coal had to be got
down or fireirons used, they were generally considered
very desirable in adverse conditions. Most of the
sheets used were left over from the wartime days when
they had been issued to all engines as a black-out
precaution, and I later discovered that nearly all Bank
Pilot and Trip link drivers owned one or more such
sheets. In extremes of weather, the main screen could
be supplemented with side curtains, and then the cab
could be made very snug indeed but these, when fitted,
generally restricted vision to such an extent that they
had to be removed when in motion.

The controller was housed in a small extension of
Duddeston Road signal box and, having mounted the steps,
Bill knocked politely on the door and entered. 'Morning
Charles,' said Bill affably. 'Any idea where 3223 is?'
'Just a minute,' returned the controller, hunting
through a heap of papers lying on the top of his desk.
'Ah yes, she only went down about twenty minutes ago, so
she should still be in the pilot sidings.' 'Righto,'
said Bill and then, turning to me, continued, 'We had
better have a gentle walk down there, mate. I don't

suppose she'll be coming out just yet.' This assumption
in fact proved correct, but we walked along the path at
the side of the intermediate line in case by chance 3223
had been called out again. I soon discovered that
talking about his local workingmen's club was Bill's
favourite topic of conversation. By the time we were
passing Saltley station I already had a fair idea of the
club's layout, decor, and the type of entertainment that
it provided. Bill continued by elaborating on the
virtues possessed by a new brand of milk stout. . . .

At length the pilot sidings came into view. On my
previous outings I had never taken much notice of them,
but now I surveyed the scene with an interested eye.
They consisted of two short roads (just sufficiently
long to each hold three Class 3Fs) which converged
before leading out to the down goods and down main.
The exit was controlled by two ground signals, one for
the goods and one for the main, while the other branch
of the points led to a short sand drag which terminated
near the top of the steep banks of a small brook.
Direct access to the sidings could only be gained from
the up Camp Hill goods line. Between the sidings and
lying under the shadow of the great brick viaduct
carrying Western Division metals there was a drab but
substantial-looking wooden hut. Our engine stood behind
another Class 3F on the rear road, while a third one
with a healthy column of black smoke erupting from its
chimney stood on the front sidings. As we approached,
the points clanked over and the upper dummy (the name by
which we called ground signals) dropped. A cloud of
steam, brilliantly reflecting the sunlight, enveloped
the fore-end of this latter Class 3F and, as the hiss
grew to a crescendo, she shuddered into motion, slipped
vigorously on the points and then pounded past us on
the down goods line in hot pursuit of the train it was
to bank. 'Blimey,' exclaimed Bill. 'Walter's in a
devil of a hurry. He must want to get past the shed
before his relief books on.' 'Does he like overtime
then?' I queried. 'Yes, he's a proper glutton for it,'
replied Bill with an air of disapproval. 'I don't mind
a spot of overtime at night when nothing's spoiling,
but I'm blowed if I'm keen at this time of day.'

I followed Bill into the cabin which, despite
external appearances, was very clean and tidy. It was
also decidedly warm, since it contained another example
of those good old cast iron stoves roaring away in the
corner. A tall, thin, sallow-complexioned driver in

his mid-fifties stood, feet apart, warming his back
against it, while another driver of about the same age,
whose features resembled those of a humorous parrot, sat
with a young fireman at the usual zinc-covered table.
The tall driver regarded me keenly with bright black,
intelligent eyes. 'Got your new mate then, Bill,' he
observed with a slight West Country drawl. Bill nodded,
and at the same time introduced me to Alf, the other
driver who was the one we were to relieve. 'She's not
too bad,' said Alf, referring to 3223. 'The left piston
gland is blowing a bit and there are a few groans at the
front end, but I've cleaned out the cylinder lubricator
and it seems to be improving now. The brake wasn't very
clever either; I've oiled it once, but I expect it will
need some more. Oh, and I've rigged a sheet up, so you
should be all right.' 'Well done,' said Bill, on
hearing this piece of good news, and with that the three
of us trooped outside and went across to our engine
where Alan, the fireman, had just finished cleaning down
the footplate. We had a quick exchange of information,
then he joined Alf on the floor and they both departed
towards the shed.

The general appearance of 3223, from the absence of
woodwork on the toolboxes to the sludge-encrusted boiler
fittings, indicated that she had not been shopped very
recently, but Alan had certainly made an effort with the
slaking pipe. The well-worn floorboards, although not
exactly white, were without doubt quite a light shade of
grey, and not a single particle of coal besmirched the
gleaming lap plate and tender front. Substantial planks
had been acquired to serve as seats which, with additional lengths to act as back-rests, looked adequately
comfortable and would no doubt be much appreciated by
the night shift. What I could see of the coal, with the
sheet in place, was typical of the lower grades used on
goods engines at that period; it burned quite well in
the fierce draught of a Class 3 firebox, but produced an
appreciable amount of ash and a soft porous type of
clinker. After depositing our belongings in the tender
locker, Bill turned to me and said with a meaningful
smile, 'By the way, that driver in there was Oliver
Birchley. He's a black belt judo expert, trains the
police in self-defence and all that, so don't ever
tangle with him.' Bill then announced that he was going
to have a check round the engine and suggested that,
since we had a few minutes, it would be a good idea if I
took this opportunity to trim the coal and clean out the

well at the back of the tender.

It seems that it was standard practice on bank pilots to remove spillage and old coal from the section behind the rear coal bulkhead around the tank filler, and also to trim the coal as low as possible on the driver's side to improve rearward vision when running tender-first. With the firing shovel grasped tightly in one hand, I wormed my way underneath the sheet and clambered over the coal to the back of the tender. There, true to form, I found there was indeed an appreciable amount of cobbles and slack, bleached to a bluish-black by prolonged exposure to light, virtually filling the well. I set to work with gusto in the crisp air, shovelling the mixture forwards, and at the same time cursing the rivet heads protruding from the steel plates forming the well, since these kept obstructing the shovel blade. In a few minutes the task was completed, and I settled the fireirons - which I noted were nearly new - more securely before returning to the footplate. Bill had just returned his oil bottles to the locker when a Class 8F with loose-sounding side rods clanked slowly past on the down goods line. By the tone of its exhaust beat it was hauling a fair load of what, as far as I could see, were all coal wagons and, as the rear of the engine drew just ahead of the sidings, a distinct single hoot came from its whistle. 'That's a Bordesley for Oliver,' commented Bill, who was also watching with interest. 'A Bordesley?' I enquired. 'A Bordesley tripper,' replied Bill a little impatiently. 'Haven't you worked one yet?' 'No,' I answered a trifle sheepishly. 'I have never been past Landor Street relief cabin.' 'Oh, well, Bordesley trippers work transfer traffic on to the Great Western at Bordesley Junction, which is only about three-quarters of a mile up the bank from Landor Street. There are dozens of 'em. In fact, I reckon there must be a Bordesley trip job in just about every bottom group road link. They're pretty cushy, not much work, and a lot of hanging around, a sort of rest between other turns; but they're usually coal trains, and heavy ones at that, which is why they are generally booked Class 8s. If unlucky, you can bank a couple of Bordesleys while one of the other blighters is lounging around up at Kings Heath.'

As the Bordesley's long train clunked slowly by, Oliver's fireman, Brian, who was one of the older hands in the link, leaped aboard his engine and started to prepare her for the work in hand. Oliver soon joined

him and, as the dummy dropped, they surged gently
forward out on to the goods line, with a fine pillar of
black smoke climbing from their chimney as a result of a
wide open blower. Seconds later, two more pilots
coupled together joined us in the sidings, and Bill
departed to have a chat with the other drivers.

Left to my own devices I decided that, since we were
next in line for duty, I had better liven up the fire,
and therefore opened the damper a couple of notches. I
was just preparing to place a few shovels of coal under
the door when the two firemen from the other pilots
scrambled on to the footplate. I knew them both from my
cleaning days and they had preceded me into the pilots
by some weeks, so I was glad of this opportunity to ply
them with questions about the link. It was soon apparent that they enjoyed piloting far more than shed work,
although they felt that the attitude some of the drivers
had towards each other and the job in general was a bit
petty. Also, some of the drivers seemed to enjoy
baiting firemen by asking all manner of questions
construed to making them feel small and incompetent.
Before the week had progressed very far, I too ran foul
of one of the drivers most practiced in this art.
Fortunately, my educational background sufficed for me
to more than hold my own on most general knowledge
subjects, and indeed tie him in knots on many matters
not pertaining to railways. This won great approval
from Bill, who did not like the fellow and, of course,
all the firemen present and thereafter I was treated
with a new respect that I enjoyed for the duration of my
stay in the link.

Our interesting discourse was suddenly interrupted in
mid-flow by a Class 4F, bearing through freight headlamps, chugging vigorously past on the down goods. 'Get
her hot!' yelled the fireman in a Gloucester dialect,
giving at the same time a friendly wave indicating that
they required a banker. A few seconds later, a shrill
pop of the whistle officially confirmed the request.
'We'll leave you to it then,' said Mike, one of my
guests, and they both departed to the cabin. I knocked
the blower hard over, fully opened the damper and
flashed a few shovels of coal evenly around the box
before partially closing the firedoors, which were of
the later sliding pattern. 'Everything all right?' said
Bill as he hauled himself up between the uprights.
'Yes, I think so,' I replied, glancing reassuringly at
the gauges which showed 160lbs. per sq.in. and nearly a

full glass of water. 'Take off the hand brake then,' he
said affably, applying the steam brake and pushing the
gear lever to the full forward position. 'And keep your
eye on the dummy.' It duly dropped and, with a hiss of
steam from the open taps, we puffed out on the goods
line in pursuit of the retreating brake van. 'There's
no need to put too much on yet,' advised Bill as I bent
to shovel more on to the grate. 'Just build it up under
the door because, as like as not, we will stand for some
time at Duddeston Road and we don't want to be blowing
off all the time.'

We caught up our train as it came to a halt outside
Saltley station and stood there for some fifteen minutes
before moving slowly to the intermediate line alongside
the down Camp Hill goods. Oliver Birchley was still in
position behind his Bordesley on that line, so obviously
the G.W.R. were not ready for them yet. 'I expect that
we will go first,' said Bill, eyeing the Bordesley
disapprovingly. 'They usually try and keep the intermediate clear if they can.' This information only
served to make me more fidgety than ever, for I was
undecided whether to put more coal on at the risk of
blowing off, and then drop the damper which might cause
the fire to set, or leave matters as they were and hope
that I could build the fire up quickly enough to meet
demands when we actually came to move. In the end I
compromised by placing a few more shovels of coal in the
back corners and leaving the damper open one notch.
During the course of time, experience showed that when
doubts existed, and they nearly always did exist
regarding the actual timing one was required to make
the assault on the bank, it was prudent to keep a fair
amount of fire in the back of the box. By leaving the
damper open a small amount and the bars thinly covered
at the front, the generation of steam whilst standing
could be effectively controlled and consequent blowing
off avoided. Even if the front of the grate went dead,
and I often allowed it to at times, the situation could
be quickly rectified by the simple expedient of digging
the blade of the firing shovel into the mass under the
doors and shooting it forwards. Generally speaking a
3F warmed up so quickly and steamed so well that
liberties like this could be readily undertaken without
detriment to performance, even with low grade fuels.

Another ten minutes passed, during which time my
eyes rarely left the signal controlling our line for
more than a few seconds. Bill, on the other hand, was

quite relaxed, sitting on his plank reading the morning
paper. I stared ahead for the umpteenth time and then,
as I watched, the signal came off. 'We're going now,
Bill,' I shouted, and without further ado pulled up the
damper and quickly flashed half a dozen shovels of coal
round the box. In contrast to my excitement, Bill
methodically folded his newspaper, transferred his
reading glasses to their protective case, slowly rose to
his feet and gently eased open the regulator. We moved
forwards a few yards before coming to a halt again, the
train crew apparently not having yet noticed the signal.
Suddenly the clank of couplings could be heard above the
background hiss of our slightly blowing piston glands,
and then we were off. Bill made no effort to open the
regulator any further, so that as we trundled steadily
up the intermediate we were pushing no more than five or
six wagons. However, as soon as we cleared the points
and were firmly on the down goods, he pushed the regulator across a trifle more and our exhaust took on a more
strident note.

Opposite the loco shed the gradient steepened to 1 in
105 and the bark from our chimney changed to that
familiar raucous crash I liked so much. I saw that Bill
had opened up to full first valve and, meeting my gaze
with a broad grin, he nodded ahead. 'We've got the back
'un now, so you can get shovelling.' A brief glance
towards the Landor Street home signal indeed confirmed
that the distant for St.Andrews Junction was also off,
so I rapidly plied more coal to the fire, which was
already taking on that white furnace glow. At Landor
Street Junction the track curves to the left and then
straightens before swinging right for the short but
steepest section of the bank, where it passes under the
main line to Euston at a gradient of 1 in 62. We were
now accelerating quite briskly before hitting this
stretch, the blast of our exhaust echoing back from the
massive G.E.C. works on our left, while up ahead a tall
pillar of smoke and steam from the Class 4 stood out
starkly against the bright blue sky, denoting that it
was certainly getting stuck in to some effect. Our own
engine was also in fine fettle, with the water just in
sight at the top of the glass, the needle on the red
line at 175 and a heavy pall of smoke keeping pace with
us overhead, carried on the following north-east breeze.
Speed progressively slackened as we approached the
Euston line bridge and, noting this, I glanced enquiringly at Bill. He read my thoughts accurately, for he

came over and bellowed in my ear. 'The whole weight of
the train is now on the steepest part. If we're going
to stick, this is where it happens, but I reckon we
shall be O.K. this time.' His statement proved to be
quite correct, for although our pace dropped to little
more than a fast walk as we blasted under the blackened
archway and past Brickyard crossing, it picked up again
on rounding the curve at St.Andrews Junction, where the
gradient eased slightly to 1 in 85.

On the straight section up to Bordesley Junction we
pounded steadily away still in full forward gear, the
exhaust amplified by the deep cutting, making a really
glorious sound. This was great stuff, I thought, as I
vigorously fired more fuel into that glaring white
orifice. The injector had been on some time now and was
just keeping the water level nicely in sight, while to
my delight the needle had not dropped below the 170
mark. The distant for Camp Hill was off but our speed
remained constant as we thundered explosively under the
wide Coventry Road bridge and past Bordesley Junction
signal box, where Bill came across and waved to the
bobby who was looking out of an open window. 'That's
Charlie Bunn. He's a pal of mine. We do well with
Bordesleys on this shift.' The significance of this
remark did not register then, for Bill went on to point
out the line leading into the Great Western system and
as we climbed still higher, we passed over the massive
viaduct which spanned the numerous G.W. tracks. The
whole Bordesley complex was laid out before us like a
huge model railway. We were now on top of a steep
embankment and a panoramic view of Birmingham was
visible to either side in the clear autumn air. Old
factories and warehouses lined a murky canal far below,
while acres of slate-grey rooftops stretched in all
directions. We then clattered over a steel bridge
spanning what I recognised was the main Stratford road
at Camp Hill and I realised that on many occasions as a
boy I had enviously watched trains puffing laboriously
over this very piece of track, never dreaming that one
day I would be actually up here on my own engine.

Our pace began to quicken noticeably, but as I once
more pounced on the shovel, Bill laid a restraining
hand on my shoulder. 'Let her go for now,' he yelled.
'We normally come off at Camp Hill box, which is just
up ahead. If he wants us up to Kings Heath, he will
whistle and the bobby will wave us through with a green
flag. Keep your eye on him and if he gives us the tip,

then you can put some more on.' I nodded to indicate
that I understood, for the noise on the footplate now
precluded normal speech, and after knocking off the
injector I stared intently ahead at the rapidly approaching signal box. The bank had now flattened from 1 in
85 to 1 in 280 and, with no adjustment in the regulator
position, our acceleration was progressive. Bill eased
off a little and then I saw the green flag, but I was
too late to advise him for he popped the whistle in
acknowledgment, at the same time hauling back the gear
lever to shorten the cut-off. I rapidly fired another
dozen shovels of coal and, as the safety valves began to
lift, put on the injector again. At 35 per cent and
just about full first regulator we fairly romped along
the easy stretch from Camp Hill to Brighton Road,
leaving an impressive trail of smoke and sound. Half
sitting on the tender hand brake bracket I experienced a
tremendous feeling of exhilaration as I swayed easily
with this wildly bucking creature, which felt full of
life and power and not at all mechanical.

Our pace began to slacken once more as the track
curved to the right and the gradient increased to 1 in
108. This was the beginning of the second step of the
climb up to Kings Heath. Moderately loaded trains
usually managed the ascent through the Moseley Tunnel
without too much trouble, provided that they had a clear
road and were able to take a run at it after Camp Hill.
Fully loaded trains, or those which for some reason were
hauled by engines not functioning as well as they might,
called for assistance right through to Kings Heath, for
sticking in a tunnel is no joke for anyone. It was very
noticeable in the course of time, however, that the
majority of Class 4F-hauled freights requested a pilot
for the full distance, which was doubtless due to the
fact that these engines in general seemed more short of
breath on the bank than any other type.

From the embankment at Brighton Road we entered a
cutting, the grassy banks of which gradually rose higher
and higher on either side until finally the plain stone
portals of the tunnel were visible. Since our speed had
now fallen considerably and the distant for Kings Heath
was off, Bill allowed the reversing lever to slam forward into full gear as we snorted vigorously into the
black mouth, which was now belching clouds of smoke and
steam left by the train engine. I later found that
Moseley Tunnel always seemed clean and lacked that
distinctive stale odour associated with many others I

was to become familiar with. This was probably due to
its location in a roughly east-west cutting, allowing
the prevailing winds to be channelled through at
increased velocity, thereby quickly clearing any residual stench. Also of course it was not an over-long
tunnel by any standards.

Bursting out into daylight once more, I found that we
were still in a deep but wide cutting that gradually
opened out on the righthand side until it revealed an
engineers' sidings located in what might have been an
old clay quarry. A number of wagons and bolster flats
containing permanent way materials stood on these rusty-
looking rails, while all around them towered precipitous
red cliffs dotted with numerous rabbit warrens. 'Nearly
there,' shouted Bill as I went over to his side to view
this spectacle. 'I shall shut off at the next bridge.'
I looked ahead and noticed an overhead road bridge
coming into sight as the track made a righthand curve
through Kings Heath station. The sharp blast of our
exhaust gently subsided as we passed under this bridge
and a prolonged application of the brake brought us to
a grinding halt at the far end of the relatively short
down platform. Although no longer in use, Kings Heath
station showed no signs of neglect; on the contrary,
it was extremely neat and tidy, sporting well-cultivated
flower beds which must have been a blaze of colour
earlier in the year, and very typical of many old
Midland country stations.

We had arrived with 160lbs. per sq.in. on the clock,
half a glass of water and only a little more fire in
the box than was strictly desirable, so I was well
pleased with my first assault of the bank. Bill also
seemed satisfied, for he chatted amiably while we
waited to see what was going to happen to us. 'Syd
Dean is the bobby on this shift,' he said, nodding
towards the box. 'Funny chap. I don't get on too well
with him, so I expect he'll shoot us back if there's
half a chance.' However, this was not to be. A few
seconds later the dummy dropped and we found ourselves
backing into the little slip road which lay parallel to
the down line at the leading end of that platform.
Once inside, Bill popped the whistle to indicate that
we were clear and trundled up to the stop block, which
was set in the embankment just below the stone pier of
the overhead bridge. With plenty of boiler space, I
was able to reduce the steam pressure to 130 without
overfilling it and, at the same time, swill away the

accumulated dirt and debris with the slaking pipe.

Some twenty minutes later another mixed freight clattered noisily through the station, followed by a pilot which halted abruptly just beyond the end of the platform, then backed gently up to us. Peter, the fireman on it, dropped in the four-foot and I watched with interest how he coupled up, for this was a task I had little experience of. First he pulled off the vacuum hoses from both engines and left them dangling, so that neither could create a vacuum to release their brakes until he had finished. Then he heaved up the heavy shackle from our engine and, after dropping it securely in the hook of his own, screwed it tight enough to remove the slack. Grasping the ends of the hoses in each hand, he deftly clipped them together with a powerful twist of his wrists, finally locking the flanges with the safety pin provided. 'O.K.,' he said with a grin, handing up our headlamp. 'Been having a nice quiet rest?' I answered in the affirmative, surprised to learn that our stay had not passed unnoticed by the other pilot crews.

Our release from the siding was simply effected by running forward on the down clear of the crossover and then proceeding back on to the up line. Being on a downward gradient of 1 in 356, only a few puffs were necessary to send the pair of us rolling easily towards the advance starter which was still on, indicating that the Class A ahead of us had not yet cleared Camp Hill. 'That white diamond with a black "T" on it means that the signal is track-circuited, but we have to telephone the bobby if detained for more than a couple of minutes, and then ring him at five-minute intervals thereafter,' said Bill. 'Come on, I'll show you how it works, because it's your job really.'

We climbed down to the base of the signal, where a weathered wooden cabinet stood on two substantial posts. Access to the instrument was gained through a small counterweighted sliding panel not unlike a miniature window sash and, holding this down with one hand, Bill lifted a single earpiece attached to a length of armoured cable off its rest with the other. Prodding the call button with a podgy forefinger, he waited a few seconds before bellowing loudly into the mouthpiece inside the cabinet. 'That's all there is to it,' he said as we returned to the footplate. 'You only have to tell him who we are, and that should remind him not to send another train into the back of us - just a question

of safety.' I was about to use the telephone again
when the whip and rustle of cables along their trackside
rollers fractionally preceded the rising of the signal
arm. Both engines accelerated impressively into the
tunnel before being allowed to coast towards Brighton
Road. I stayed mainly on Bill's side so as to view the
scenery I had missed on the way up, the keen air blowing
in round the sheet and making my eyes water. The
distant for Camp Hill was off as it came into sight and,
since there was nothing to be gained in dawdling, Bill
opened up again. As our speed rose, small particles of
coal and dust from the tender were picked up in the airstream and peppered us unpleasantly at both face level
and about the shins where they blew in from the
shovelling plate. After this experience I always well
soaked the coal before running tender-first, for to try
it when already in motion was both futile and very wet.
On this section from Camp Hill to Bordesley it became
obvious how easily the Class 3s coasted; they ran
freely and steadily, with very little noise other than
a distinctive double-three click of wheels over rail
joints.

We were halted at Bordesley Junction and while
standing there an 8F hauling a heavy coal train thumped
explosively from under the Coventry Road bridge and
pounded towards us. A towering mushroom of black smoke
was being hurled skywards from the chimney at each
tremendous beat and the volume of sound was absolutely
deafening as it blasted slowly past. Because she
seemed to be working so much harder than normal I
peered intently to see where the regulator was set and,
not surprisingly, noted that it was dead horizontal.
'That's the way to do it,' I shouted at Bill, pulses
atingle at the sight of this demonstration of power.
'Wish they all would,' he agreed, apparently quite
unmoved. 'Makes life easier for us.' The banker was
also well extended, its crisp exhaust note crackling to
and fro in the brick-lined cutting as it emerged from
the bridge, surrounded by steam and smoke. I had been
counting the heavy coal wagons as they thumped over the
rail joints opposite and observed that the pilot was
pushing seventeen out of the total of fifty. I often
found myself doing this exercise, and it soon became
apparent that a Class 3 on full first valve and in full
gear averaged about this quantity on the bank. Bill
came over to see who was on the pilot and exchanged a
hasty greeting with Oliver Birchley, who was hanging

his lanky form well out of the cab. 'I reckon he'll be
going through to Kings Heath with that lot,' said Bill.
   Our signal came off and we rolled steadily down to
St.Andrews Junction, where we stood for some considerable while, and so I was obliged to go to the signal box
in order to carry out Rule 55. This simple but
necessary regulation was a very frequent occurrence in
the pilot link and, as a result, I came to know the
various signalmen quite well, since I generally remained
in the box after signing the log until it was time to
move off. They were as interesting and as varied in
character as were any other breed of men and I spent
many pleasant interludes in their company when the bank
was on the block.
   The Class A preceding us had halted at Brickyard
crossing, which I found was not at all unusual, since
many trains took on water at the column at Landor Street
Junction, the next block ahead, this being also a relief
point. Eventually it moved on and Bill stopped outside
the box to allow me to join him once again. 'We had
better get some water ourselves at Landor Street,' said
Bill, nodding towards the tank gauge which now showed
less than 1,500 gallons. 'Charlie is O.K., but we may
not get another chance for a while.' By the time we
had watered our engine the Class A had disappeared,
giving us a clear run down to Duddeston Road. Twenty
minutes later I was uncoupling our engines in the pilot
siding where, at Bill's suggestion, I tackled the job of
getting some coal forward. Moving coal from the rear of
the tender towards the front is an onerous operation
until one digs down to the tank top; then once one has
found this flat platform to work from it is merely a
case of some strenuous shovelling. It was an unwritten
law in the pilots that the day shift did as much of this
as possible, because the job was rendered much more
difficult in the dark and we tried to make life as easy
as possible for our colleagues on nights.
   Half an hour later a Class 8 struggled by and hooted
for a pilot. It was our turn once more and, having by
now heaped a good supply of fuel in the front half of
the tender, I quickly descended to the footplate in
order to set about livening up the fire. The first
thirty wagons of the train were loaded with coal, while
the remaining twenty appeared to be carrying pig iron,
and a full complement at that, judging by the way the
springs were flattened. Before the brake van had gone
past, Bill joined me. 'It's a Bordesley, I think,' he

said, with a note of satisfaction in his voice.
'Charlie will draw ahead first and shunt on to the rear
road,' he added, answering the question I was about to
ask as to how we were going to get out. The operation
was accomplished as planned and we duly caught our train
opposite Saltley carriage sidings where, pushing little
more than the brake van, we chugged gently on without
stopping until coming to a halt on the down Camp Hill
goods line at Duddeston Road. Here we remained for some
forty minutes, during which time we took the opportunity
to have our lunch while watching both Charlie and
another pilot run past us on the intermediate, pushing
their respective trains up the bank. At last our signal
came off and with tissues fully restored after consuming
my sandwiches, I briskly fired a dozen shovels of coal
round the box. Right from the start Bill got stuck in
with more purpose than on the previous train, since not
only were we on a straight road with no facing points to
cross, but we also had a much heavier load. However,
our acceleration was lethargic, to say the least, while
frequent surges and intermittent eruptions of smoke from
our train engine indicated that it was slipping badly.

The distants were off for St.Andrews, so Bill had no
compunction about using full first regulator and full
gear, but as we blasted past Landor Street signal box
even I could sense we were not going as well as we
should and I was not entirely surprised when he growled
in my ear, 'If the chaps up front don't do better than
this we will most certainly stick.' I could see the
smoke and steam from the Class 8 billowing up beyond
Brickyard crossing, indicating that it was now on the
steepest section of the bank, and this could be felt on
our own engine by a gradual falling off in speed. As
the resistance increased, 3223 began to perform little
half slips which Bill quickly checked by opening the
sand valve. We were just nearing the Euston line overbridge and our pace had dropped to nothing more than a
crawl. The exhaust beats, having lost their sharp
clear crackle, now became long drawn-out muffled woofs.
Bill pushed the regulator right across, but it was of
no avail and with a prolonged sigh of resignation we
shuddered to a standstill. 'That's it, then,' said
Bill in a tone just as resigned as the engines. 'Screw
the hand brake on, mate.' I did so, and as Bill
released the steam brake we set back several wagon
lengths under the weight of the train. The guard was
already down on the ground shouting to us. 'I'll go

and tell the bobby we want some more assistance,' he
yelled. 'Righto,' replied Bill and then, turning to me,
he said, 'We just sit tight now until another engine
comes.'

Before assistance arrived in the form of Oliver
Birchley, a full ten minutes went by, during which we
spent most of the time blowing off since I did not wish
to overfill the boiler. Returning to the pilot sidings
from Kings Heath, he had been conveniently passing the
loco at the right time and the controller quickly
arranged for him to be shunted across to the down goods,
and up behind us. Oliver's mate coupled up while I
removed our taillamp and placed his headlamp facing
inwards on the framing. 'Short of steam?' he chided,
with a good-natured grin. 'On the contrary, we've got
too much,' I replied, as the valves lifted again with a
roar, and then shouting so as to be heard above the din,
'I think the blighter up front is having a job to keep
his feet, and there's a great load of pig iron down this
end.' He waved his hand in acknowledgment and we both
returned to our respective footplates.

'O.K., Bill,' I yelled, winding off the hand brake
while he blew a couple of crow whistles to indicate to
the train engine that we were ready to start pushing.
Unfortunately, a reply could not be heard, so Bill and
Oliver opened up in unison, but it was like trying to
move a mountain and both 3s started slipping violently.
These two drivers had obviously done this many times
before, since they acted as one without any signals
passing between them. With sanders running, we set
back until all the slack was out of the train couplings,
and then on full first valve we charged into the wagons
with no attempt at gentleness or concern for the guard's
hide. To begin with we literally raced forwards, but as
the train buffered up the weight of each wagon could be
felt as a distinct check, rather like shunting, until
after a few yards and still on the approach side of the
bridge we came nearly to a standstill again. Once more
Bill pushed the regulator right across, and judging by
the bark from Oliver's chimney he had done likewise.
Then, with a shudder of triumph, we surged ahead under
the bridge and up to St.Andrews. With both pilots fully
extended, the noise in the cutting was as shattering as
it was exhilarating, and as the train passed on to the
1 in 85 stretch, our speed had risen sufficiently to
allow Bill to come back on the first regulator.
Although we had long since had a clear road right into

Bordesley, we took things very cautiously once the train
was on the curve leading to the Great Western. With
such a weighty load, stopping at the signal there would
be enough of a problem without any unwelcomed pushing
from us.

Despite Bill's alleged friendship with the bobby we
were quickly shunted across to the up goods for a speedy
return to Landor Street. We concluded that they must be
short of pilots and this was in fact borne out, for at
Saltley Junction we were detached from Oliver and
directed behind a through freight standing on the down
Camp Hill line. I had only just enough time to build up
the fire a little when we were off again, but by way of
a contrast this train was lightly loaded and we fairly
romped over the stretch leading to St.Andrews Junction.
Having a good charge at the bank made a great deal of
difference, and speed did not fall too significantly on
the 1 in 62 section. However, it soon became apparent
that 3223 was not steaming as well as she had earlier
in the day, and I was having to sacrifice the water
level in the boiler after passing Bordesley Junction.
Fortunately the train engine did not require us through
to Kings Heath, for as we ground to a halt just beyond
the old disused Camp Hill station platform we had no
more than half a glass of water and 140lbs. per sq.in.
showing on the clock. 'I reckon that you've got some
clinker in there, mate,' said Bill after we had backed
inside the short slip road. 'I reckon that you're
right,' I replied, inspecting the offending fire. 'I'll
clean it as soon as we get back to the pilot sidings.'
'When it's cooled down you can start right here if you
wish,' went on Bill. 'In fact, the way things are moving
at the moment it may be your only chance.' 'What if we
have to go back when I'm right in the middle of cleaning
it?' I stammered, somewhat surprised at this suggestion.
'That's all right,' replied Bill, quite unruffled.
'It's downhill, isn't it?' Well, there was no argument
to that, so after untying the ropes securing our sheet
and rolling it over the roof I pulled the fireirons
forward in readiness. There was rather more live coal
in the box than was really desirable, but by the time
the boiler had filled I was able to make a start. It
was not surprising that the old girl had been short of
breath this last trip, for a large slab of thick
clinker, topped with a layer of ashes, covered the rear
half of the grate. What was surprising was that she
had steamed at all in this condition; more proof, if

any was needed, of the reserve capacity built into these
engines.

As it happened, I had plenty of time to make quite a
respectable job of the cleaning operation before we were
required to depart in the company of two more pilots on
their way back from Kings Heath. After sweating profusely over my labours I found the return trip decidedly
chilly, but this was one of the occupational hazards to
which footplatemen were constantly exposed, and no doubt
the cause of many of the bouts of muscular rheumatism,
fibrositis, etc., which afflicted both young and old
alike from time to time. As Bill aptly summed it up,
'What do you expect when you are standing all day on
damp and draughty floorboards, roasted on one side and
frozen on the other?' We did manage to get to the pilot
sidings this time, although one of the other engines
accompanying us had to depart almost immediately.
However, the brief respite there enabled me to complete
the task of getting coal forward and make a thorough job
of cleaning down the footplate.

At 3.15 we found ourselves behind another Bordesley
and Bill peering anxiously at his pocket watch. 'Our
relief books on at 4.00,' he mumbled, half to himself.
'We don't want to be going past the shed at that time,
or goodness knows when we'll be finished.' Bill
obviously did not want any overtime on this shift and
would be glad to be relieved outside the shed. Ironic-
ally, half the other drivers would be only too pleased
to sneak past and then have an hour inside at Kings
Heath. He need not have worried. It took the best
part of an hour for the train engine to get to Duddeston
Road, and we were still standing at the rear of it on
the down Camp Hill goods when our relief climbed aboard
at 4.25 p.m. They were very happy, not having had a
long walk, and Bill likewise was delighted, since he
could not have been relieved sooner.

During the week, I had become familiar with the bank,
its landmarks, its gradients, the various types of
trains working on it, when and where the main effort was
made as well as when and where to run the fire and
boiler down. This knowledge, of course, was necessary
if one was to work efficiently, and towards the end of
the week I had gained sufficient confidence to experiment with my firing technique. Carrying too much fire
around meant not only extra work firing, but the
possibility of blowing off excessively, which in turn
led to wasting water. The more coal fired, the more one

had to shovel forward on the tender, and carrying a big
fire meant that it got dirtier more quickly, particularly if the damper was being closed frequently.
Therefore, in order to save my back as much as to save
the company expense, I tried firing lighter and lighter
until I reached the point where holes were being
dragged in the firebed to the detriment of good
steaming. However, this point was much lower than I
originally supposed, and with 3223 the ideal seemed to
be having it just below the mouthpiece ring at the back,
sloping evenly down to a thickness of only two or three
inches at the front. She was very tolerant to different
methods though, and if one overdid things, either with
too much firing or too little, the needle would quickly
respond to corrective measures. It was in any case
difficult to get into much trouble on that four-mile
stretch in the normal way, for if the train took a few
minutes longer from point to point due to the pilot
driver easing up, it was difficult to apportion blame.

The following week we booked on at 4.00 p.m. and I
was quite looking forward to my first taste of night
work on the pilots. After bright sunshine during the
day, fog was beginning to form as I cycled to work. We
went through the now-familiar procedure of ascertaining
the whereabouts of our engine, and found that it was
conveniently standing behind a Class B on the down Camp
Hill goods some five minutes later. We relieved our
colleagues, who were anxiously awaiting our arrival and
obviously keen to set off home. 'She's O.K., apart
from the injector clack sticking sometimes,' said Syd,
the driver, more to me than to Bill, and then as an
afterthought as he climbed down the steps, 'We've
got you some good seats.' They had indeed, for there
were enough planks on the toolbox lockers to build a
small shed, and would be very much appreciated during
the night if the chance came to have a quick snooze.
I tried the offending injector, but it seemed to function perfectly well; however, as a precaution I kept
a spanner handy just in case I had to persuade the
clack valve to drop with a sharp tap to the top of the
box. This was the unofficial method enginemen adopted
should it stick, a method unpopular with the fitters
since it distorted the access nut on the top of the
clack box, but with an uncontrollable jet of steam
blowing out of the injector overflow pipe one had no
time for engineering finesse.

The light was now failing fast, and because fog was

settling down on the scene one could barely see more
than 150 yards. 'You'd better light the lamps while
you've got the chance,' advised Bill, opening the tool
locker and taking out the canister of detonators. 'Just
making sure that we've got some - by the look of things,
we may need them tonight.' I climbed down and lit our
head- and taillamps, and as I returned to the footplate
I noticed that Bill was stuffing a couple of potatoes
behind the clack box of his injector. He then packed
them well into place with a cloth and proceeded to do
the same thing with a large onion on my injector. 'If
you keep turning them every half-hour or so, they will
be nicely done in time for supper,' he explained. I
must admit that I had not seen this form of cooking
before, and the thoughts of some warm food on a winter's
night prompted me to do likewise in the future. It was
virtually dark by the time we set off up the bank and,
although visibility was no worse than earlier, I was
amazed how lost I felt. Distinguishing landmarks could
no longer be seen and at the time I did not know the
bank well enough to visualise every yard of it in my
mind's eye. However, Bill seemed quite unaffected by
the conditions, although he did come over to my side to
check the distant for Camp Hill.

As is often the case with mist or fog, it tended to
form in the hollows and on the low ground first, so that
beyond Camp Hill we only had the dark to contend with.
At first I found working on the footplate at night somewhat disturbing, inasmuch as the extremes of lighting
were initially difficult to adjust to. From virtually
complete blackness other than the small guttering flame
of the gauge lamp, there was sudden transformation to
blinding white light on opening the firedoors. Nor was
this illumination diffused in any way, for the matt
black surfaces inside the cab reflected very little
light, so that it was rather like being in the beam of a
searchlight. It took quite some time before I adjusted
to these conditions, but gradually the adaptation came
about.

We were detained for about forty minutes at Kings
Heath and here, although there was no trace of fog and
little wind, the air was decidedly cold and the first
traces of frost began to twinkle on the sleepers in the
dim lighting. We had no cab sheet and I found that it
soon became necessary to stand in front of the open
firedoors at intervals to keep warm. Descending the
bank again coupled to another pilot, I was very glad of

the thick, company-issue reefer jacket, for there was no
shelter from the wind caused by our motion as we travelled tender-first. On the embankment between Camp Hill
and Bordesley, we once more looked out over the sea of
fog which appeared to be at rooftop level and glowed
eerily from the illumination of countless street lamps.
Thrusting up into the clear air above could be seen the
tops of the tall buildings and church spires which
abound in that area. At Bordesley we plunged into the
fog, but it was not thick enough to impede our progress
unduly, although I found it just sufficiently dense to
tax my memory and knowledge to the limit. Indeed it was
to prove a useful introduction to the old-fashioned
pea-soupers which we experienced later in the week. The
evening, while fairly busy, turned out to be quite
routine and, weather-wise, conditions remained more or
less constant. Bill devoured his potatoes and onion
during a lengthy wait at Camp Hill and pronounced them
to be very toothsome indeed, a fact which had not
escaped my notice. We were at Kings Heath when our
relief booked on, and it was a further hour and a half
before they eventually climbed aboard at Landor Street
Junction, but as Bill exclaimed, 'Nothing was spoiling
at that hour of the morning, and we were after all being
paid time and a half.'

The following day, Tuesday, was fine and sunny and
the evening quite clear, although extremely cold for
that time of the year. On Wednesday morning, however,
fog descended again, so I decided to set off to work
somewhat earlier than usual. Visibility had closed down
to between fifteen and twenty yards, the fog taking on
that yellow-grey colour which portends a real thick one,
and by the time I had parked my cycle in the racks I was
relying entirely on memory as to where to find the shed
entrance. Bill was already in the lobby when I entered
and from his expression seemed relieved to see me.
'You've got here all right, then?' he queried. 'Yes,'
I replied, wiping droplets of moisture from my hair and
eyebrows, 'but it's getting a bit dodgy outside now.'
He nodded sombrely. 'Here, put these in your bag. I
reckon we'll need a few extra tonight,' and he handed
me a cardboard box containing twelve detonators.

We made our way outside again, where the fog clouds
were rolling in thicker than ever and we could see no
more than ten or fifteen yards. Sound travels rather
better in fog, and because a strange eerie silence had
also settled over the area, noises a long way off

seemed quite close. We proceeded gingerly to the
control box at Duddeston Road, relying more on our ears
than our eyes to keep out of the way of traffic moving
on and off the shed, while already we could hear the
sharp crack of fog signals exploding from many different
points. 'Yours is somewhere on the way up from the
pilot sidings,' said the controller, 'but I'm having a
job to see the engine numbers in this blasted lot.' We
could readily appreciate that point, for even on the
intermediate line just in front of the box engines were
now appearing as only vague dark shapes. Keeping close
to the gas works boundary fence, we cautiously headed
towards the pilot sidings, listening intently for all
signs of movement and at the same time peering continuously around our own little grey world which extended
in a radius no more than ten yards or so. The engine
number on the banker at the rear of a train on the down
Camp Hill could not be distinguished until we were
virtually standing at the bottom of its steps, and then
it was the driver's voice which first told us that it
was not ours. A passenger train could be heard
vigorously snorting away from the starter on the down
main at Saltley Junction - a sure sign that things were
getting bad, if expresses were being checked or their
drivers were missing signals.

We eventually found our engine behind a westbound
mixed freight headed by a 4F, just beyond Saltley
station. Although not yet quite dark, I noticed that
the lamps had been lighted and both Syd, the driver, and
Jack, the fireman, were obviously looking out for us.
'It's come down quick today,' said Syd gravely. 'Could
get bad later in the night. I think we'll get off,' he
continued. 'You are all right in the rear; there's a
Class B standing behind the tender.' He was, of course,
referring to the chances of being run into from the rear
while standing on a road where the permissive block
system was operating, a not uncommon occurrence in foggy
conditions.

After conducting the usual preliminary checks we
settled down, placing our potatoes in suitable positions
for a gentle baking, while speculating on what might be
in store for us. A slight clank caused me to glance
ahead and I was just in time to see the brake van lights
of our train receding into the limits of visibility
which lay only a little way beyond the smokebox door.
Bill was not caught napping and eased the regulator open
instantly, but even so we travelled quite a few yards

before making contact with the brake van again. With
just sufficient steam on to maintain position, we waited
for the train engine to stop us, and when this eventually took place we found ourselves standing on the
intermediate line. 'Go and drop a detonator on the
track about twenty yards behind us,' said Bill. 'We
don't want anyone spilling our tea.' Listening intently
and taking great care not to be run down, I placed the
metal disc on top of the nearest rail, securing it in
position with the lead strips provided for the purpose.
I could hear what I took to be the Class B chugging
towards me, so I scampered back to Bill to advise him
what was happening. Seconds later a loud crash, seemingly right beneath the tender, made us both jump and we
braced ourselves instinctively. There was no need,
though, for the Class B shut off immediately and rolled
up to our tender buffers with hardly a shudder. 'It
gives the other fellow a chance and us some peace of
mind,' explained Bill, well pleased with the outcome.

      We waited some ten minutes, during which time neither
of us took our eyes off the brake ahead for more than a
few seconds, before the familiar clank of couplings
being drawn taut and a slight surge indicated that the
train was on the move again. Bill had just been
explaining that had we been on the down Camp Hill and
likely to be involved in a long wait, he would have got
me to place a detonator under the brake van wheel
(having first advised the guard) so that constant
vigilance would not have then been necessary. He
proceeded very cautiously with little more than a breath
of steam on for, in the gathering darkness, the fog
seemed denser than ever and we did not know for certain
if we had the road. Keeping the firedoors tightly
closed to prevent back glare, we both stood on my side
of the footplate, straining to catch a glimpse of the
signals at Duddeston Road. Not until we were almost
directly beneath them did we just manage to see the
double green of both the home signal with the distant
for Landor Street below it. Bill now opened up more
confidently while I added more fuel to the fire, trying
hard not to become dazzled by the brilliant white light.
He was soon over on my side again, intent on checking
the distant under the Landor Street starter, for as
long as we could see that the distants were off we
could keep going. Miss one and we would have to be
prepared to come to a stand at the next stop signal.
Because of our leisurely start we had not worked up

much speed but, as soon as Bill sighted the distant for
Brickyard crossing, he pushed the regulator right across
and our exhaust thundered out into the heavy atmosphere
like so much gunfire. He could not possibly have seen
me raise a quizzical eyebrow, but he answered my
unspoken question nevertheless. 'We don't want to stick
in this lot, and we're struggling a bit at the moment.'
With our engine, 3507, doing more than its full share,
we managed to keep going over the worst section between
Brickyard crossing and St.Andrews without actually
coming to a standstill, but one good slip and we would
have done so. Unlike Monday night, we did not run out
of the fog at Bordesley Junction; in fact, it seemed to
be getting thicker than ever, but I was able to sight
the distant for Camp Hill on the approach side of the
Coventry Road overbridge. The junction box was quite
invisible and from there on I became completely lost
over the lengthy stretch up to Camp Hill. Bill had
reverted to the first valve once past St.Andrews and
now he eased the regulator still further and took up
position on my side of the cab again, straining his eyes
into the murk ahead. 'We're coming up to the Camp Hill
home signal,' he murmured without averting his gaze.
'I expect he'll want us through with this load, but
we'll have a job to see the bobby.'
    This distant was off, but Bill did not open up again.
He was quite content just to maintain our slow and
steady pace. I peered into the blanket of fog swirling
round the engine, unable to discern a thing except for
the faint glow of the brake van taillamps, but Bill
apparently knew exactly where he was because right on
cue he leaned out between the uprights. 'Only a few
yards now,' he said. Seconds later we saw a diffused
patch of light looking like a ghostly apparition come
into view and there, leaning out of the open window, was
the bobby waving a green lamp. Bill popped the whistle
in acknowledgment, pulled the gear lever back a couple
of notches and pushed the regulator on to full first
valve. We gathered speed on the following easy grade,
but once again I was hopelessly lost until the colour
light signal at Brighton Road flashed past. It was then
that I realised how much more effective these powerful
electric signals were in fog; not only did they emit a
much brighter beam, but the lens was also closer to
one's eye level.
    We were into Moseley Tunnel before I realised it and,
once through, Bill gradually eased off so that the train

had already left us by the time we clattered under the
Kings Heath overbridge and came to a standstill alongside the down platform. 'You'd better walk back to the
box,' said Bill, 'and find out what he's going to do
with us.' I stepped blindly on to the platform and
stumbled off in what I thought was the correct direction
until, like a moth, I was able to home in on the dim
light that served to illuminate it. Banging my shins on
the short flight of steps, I entered. 'Gosh, it's black
out there, Frank,' I exclaimed, ruefully rubbing the
injured limb. 'Aye, lad,' replied Frank, who was
nearing retirement and who hailed from northern parts.
'It's a real old-fashioned pea-souper, to be sure.' I
signed the book while he continued. 'I've got a path
for you right now, so you can tell your mate to set back
as soon as he's ready. There's no sense in hanging
about in this lot.' 'O.K.,' I replied and stepped once
more into the wall of darkness outside the box. My
brief exposure to even that dim lighting left me almost
blind and I shuffled very slowly along the platform,
guided purely by the gentle hiss of our engine. I did
not spot the taillamp until only about five paces away
and just remembered in time to remove its red shade and
place it in what was formerly our headlight. 'Right,
Bill,' I said as I groped my way back to the footplate.
'He's going to have us straight back down the bank
again, and he's ready when you are.' Bill popped the
whistle and we chuffed gently over the crossover on to
the up line, just spotting that both home and distant
signals were off as we passed by. With the firedoors
tightly closed I could not see a thing, and I certainly
did not envy Bill his job of driving in these conditions
but, as before, he showed not the slightest concern,
such was his knowledge of the road.

As we coasted down towards Brighton Road, I asked
Bill how he knew so accurately where we were at any
particular point, and he explained that it was quite
simply done by observing certain lineside features such
as bridges, and then counting anything visible like
telegraph poles or quarter-mile posts, etc. Needless
to say, this required a vast amount of experience and a
memory like an elephant. We were brought to a halt at
the Camp Hill home signal, which could only just be
seen when the tender buffers were level with the post.
Conditions were definitely getting worse, for after
fifteen minutes we heard the clang of the signal coming
off, but could not see it from the footplate, so I

climbed on top of the tender to get a better view. The
extra elevation was just sufficient for me to confirm
that it was in fact safe to proceed. Bill did not go
forward to the starter but stopped opposite the signal
box - at least I had to take his word that we were
opposite the box, because it was not remotely visible
from the up line. 'Go and see the bobby and find out if
the starter is off,' said Bill. 'It will be easier than
trying to sight the damn thing in this.'

I did as requested, first listening intently in case
anything was approaching on the down line, but under the
heavy cloak of fog Camp Hill was as silent as the prov-
erbial grave. Setting off at right angles to the track,
I groped my way over rails and point rods until, after
tripping over a cluster of signal wires, I came up
against the base of the box. Once again Bill had been
dead on target. Following the wall, I eventually found,
and climbed, the long flight of steps. 'Thought you
might come up,' said the bobby cheerfully when I had
announced myself. 'I could hear you stop, but I can't
see a thing past the windows. The starter is off,' he
continued, 'but be prepared to stop at Bordesley.
There's a Class B in front of you.' I thanked him for
the information and, after nearly descending the steps
in one, I conveyed the news to Bill.

We set off cautiously and I must admit that neither
of us saw the starter light, only the post, for being
quite a tall signal it was completely lost to view. I
noticed after a short while that Bill was now leaning
over the side all the time, striving to glimpse some
point of recognition, and when I joined him on his side
of the footplate he shook his head resignedly. 'Well,
mate, I've never seen it worse than this. I can't even
make out the sleepers.' This was indeed so. One could
hardly see across the cab, let alone what was outside.
Because of this Bill, with the engine coasting at just a
crawl, was relying entirely on the different sounds it
made over the rails to pinpoint our position, an incredible feat of memory. 'Can't be far away now,' he
murmured a trifle uncertainly. 'I'll climb up on to the
back of the tender,' I volunteered, glad at last to be
of some practical assistance. Scrambling on all fours
over the coal I eventually found the well and stood
upright peering out into a solid wall of fog like some
ancient mariner. 'Nothing yet,' I called, glancing
round, and then I had a shock, for I could not even see
halfway along the tender. We crept forwards for a few

more yards and then Bill, realising the hopelessness of
our situation, stopped and called me down. 'Take my
torch and walk along the track,' he said. 'It's about
the only way we are going to find it.' By shining the
beam directly down I could just see the ground and,
after stumbling on for about ten paces without finding
anything, I shouted for Bill to follow. I continued for
another thirty yards in this manner before I suddenly
blundered into the signal post. 'Stop, Bill, I've found
it,' I called. Bill halted, and joined me at the base
of the signal. 'Is it off?' he asked optimistically.
'Blowed if I know,' I replied, shining the torch on the
post and illuminating a small area only a few feet above
our heads. 'Can you tell by the position of the count-
erweight?' 'I wouldn't like to guess,' replied Bill.
'No, there's only one thing for it, you'll have to climb
up and have a look.'

I found the slender iron ladder used by the lamp men
for servicing purposes and started to ascend. Until
then I had never realised what ricketty structures
signal posts were, for it swayed alarmingly at every
step, and when I gained the narrow slatted platform I
was surprised how large the signal arms were at close
range. 'It's on,' I called down to Bill. 'Well, you'd
better stay up there for a while. I'll go back and put
a detonator down. It will help the next chap, even
though it's not strictly necessary here.' His disem-
bodied voice floated up out of the murk below, as I
leaned back against the protective rail and took stock
of the situation. Suddenly, violent shaking almost
dislodged me from my precarious foothold as the signal
came off with a force that left both the post and I
swaying and shuddering to and fro. I waited for the
tremors to subside before slithering thankfully down
the ladder and making my way back to the engine, where
Bill was groping around with arms outstretched, trying
to find the steps. We rolled cautiously down to the
starter where we carried out the same procedure, only
on this occasion I found the signal already off.
St.Andrews home did not present quite such a problem
since, because of the overhead bridges, the signals
were set more or less at cab level and I was able to
see them from the back of the tender. Finding the box
in order to carry out Rule 55 was both difficult and
hazardous, but the bobby did not allow Bill to proceed
until the road was clear to Brickyard crossing, so once
again we could pass the starter with confidence.

Because of its close proximity, the box at Brickyard was
easier to find and when we were finally allowed down to
Landor Street, the glow from the relief cabin just
warned us in time that we were near to the signals.
After filling the tank, we had a long wait before the
bobby advised Bill - who had joined him in the box -
that the section to Duddeston Road was clear. Normally
trains are allowed to follow each other down under the
permissive system, but in these conditions no such risks
were being taken. We had travelled no more than fifty
yards when we were startled by the explosion of a detonator under our tender wheels. Bill instantly brought us
nearly to a standstill. 'Probably left by the guard on
the last train that was here,' he said, 'but keep your
eyes skinned just in case.' In fact, I could not see
past the end of the tender, but at less than walking
pace we were not likely to cause much damage. The fog
signalmen were now out in force, and the friendly glow
from their well-filled braziers did much to restore
one's confidence. However, despite their efforts and
the fact that very little traffic seemed to be moving,
it took another two hours to reach the haven of our
pilot sidings. Two other pilots were already standing
on the back road and with the chaotic conditions prevailing, it was not entirely surprising that we were
still there when our relief finally arrived at 12.45 a.m.

Early in January I was involved in an innocent little
episode that received some minor publicity in the local
press. It was a Saturday and I was working the day
shift once more. We had experienced the first appreciable fall of snow of the winter during the early hours
of that morning and when I booked on, some eight inches
lay deep and crisp and even over the entire area. It
seemed to me that it brought about a distinct
improvement to Birmingham in general and Saltley in
particular, for the acres of grimy industrial eyesores
were all now discreetly covered by this pure white
blanket. I've always been fascinated by the pictorial
transformation snow brings to any scene, and nowhere is
this more apparent than in a railway view involving a
steam locomotive at work. For one thing, all that can
be seen of the track itself is two parallel black lines,
while both engine and stock stand out from the white
backcloth with a clarity of definition not normally
observable in any other circumstances. However, it is
the way that the exhaust of steam and smoke shows up so
magnificently that impresses most. The cold air

condenses every last molecule, so that even a single
puff expands to enormous proportions and hangs in a
glorious white cloud. Likewise, every atom of carbon
stands out in stark contrast and forms beautiful rolling
patterns while entrapped in the steam. Apart from the
snow, which was not really deep enough to affect rail
traffic, the Saturday in question was progressing more
or less on routine lines until in the early afternoon,
when we were requested by the bobby at Duddeston Road
to run up behind a westbound mineral train which had
stuck at Brickyard crossing. The rails were wet and
greasy and the mineral, hauled by a Class 8F, was
exceptionally heavy, having literally slipped itself to
a stand at the usual place. Bill, grumbling about doing
an extra turn, shunted across to the down Camp Hill
while I quickly set about the task of rallying both fire
and boiler for the unexpected job ahead.

In those post-war austerity days, one could never
guarantee what type or quality of coal would be
delivered to the shed, and a couple of days previously
a trainload of ovoids had arrived. We frequently had
ovoids and bricquettes, but usually these were mixed
with normal coal. On this occasion no coal was available for mixing, however, and since the ovoids had to be
used, every freight engine at Saltley was running on a
pure diet of the things. As previously explained,
there is nothing basically wrong with ovoids; being
egg-size they burn fast and are ideal for firing over
the bottom flap of the old Midland firedoors. They do
produce, though, a lot of dust and a fantastic amount
of smoke. By the time we buffered up to the pilot
ahead I had baled in a fair quantity of them in an
effort to build up the fire at the back of the box, and
already a rich column of black smoke was billowing skywards, despite wide open firedoors and the blower hard
on. Len, the fireman on the other pilot, also got busy
with the shovel and soon his smoke was matching my own.
Bill opened the whistle to give the distinctive crow
indicating that we were ready this end and, after
receiving an answering hoot from the train engine,
allowed us to roll back a few wagon lengths before
opening the regulator onto full first valve. I
whipped up the bottom flap of the firedoors and joined
Bill on his side so that I could watch the spectacle of
our three engines getting the heavy train underway.
Both pilots slipped before the sanders took effect
while up ahead a gigantic pillar of jet black smoke

confirmed that the 8F was also on ovoids.

The slipping really livened up our fires, so that the smoke became denser than ever and, as I looked forwards, I could see Len's grinning face nodding at the triple columns of smoke and steam mushrooming up against the pure white background - a most impressive sight indeed. We clawed our way slowly past St.Andrews Junction and, as we thumped up the cutting towards the Coventry Road overbridge, I realised we could well be invited through to Kings Heath, so I started ladling ovoids in over the bottom flap as fast as I could shovel. When I looked out again we were just approaching the city football ground and, though no great enthusiast, I recalled that the Blues had an important home match on that day. A vast pall of dense black smoke and billowing clouds of steam had been left in the cutting by the Class 8 and, wafted by the faintest of breezes, it was now rolling gently over the boundary wall of the stadium. A spasm of devilment caught me and I quickly closed the top firedoor flap, which until now I had left open in order to burn some of the smoke without admitting too much cold air. Len must have had the same idea, for there was naught to choose between the vast towering pillars of black oily smoke erupting from our chimneys. It was a fantastic sight, this tremendous volume of smoke held captive by the cold heavy atmosphere, following and reinforcing the smokescreen laid by the train engine. Of its effect we knew nothing although, even above the crash of the twin exhaust, I thought I heard the roar of the crowd just before passing under the Coventry Road bridge. I had forgotten the incident until, when booking off that evening in the lobby, I happened to glance over the shoulder of a fireman reading the Sports Argus. There in bold print was the heading of the report on Birmingham's game. 'Mid-match black-out! The Blues gained a slender 1-0 victory today when they scored a controversial goal just after half-time when play was temporarily blotted out by smoke and steam drifting in from the nearby railway line. . . . ' I read no more and, pulling my collar well up, crept quickly away. . . .

With the coming of spring, I had acquired a fair working knowledge of the bank and, although I say it myself, I could provide more than enough steam on a Class 3F. Moreover, Bill was allowing me to drive the engine on return trips down bank, and when feeling in need of a little exercise, also occasionally handed over

for the real business too. Looking back, I had been
extremely happy in the pilots. I had advanced my firing
technique to a very considerable degree, and had become
thoroughly familiar with a 3F from both sides of the
footplate, even to the extent of oiling it from stem to
stern. I had also gained a sound knowledge of that
section of line between Washwood Heath and Kings Heath,
apart from acquiring the countless little snippets of
information that go towards making an engineman generally competent in discharging his duties. The training
had been indeed most useful and an ideal stepping stone
for greater things to come, so that when the annual May
reshuffle arrived I looked forward to expanding my
horizons with eager anticipation.

VI

THE CONTROL LINK

The great advantage of the Control link was that one rarely knew what one was going to do from day to day. As previously explained, there were no booked jobs, only booked times, and after signing on one just waited until something turned up. As often as not, this was no more inspiring a duty than walking across to Landor Street relief cabin and waiting an hour or two for some train that terminated at Washwood Heath up sidings. Or by way of a change one might go to Bromford and work the mile or so to the West End. Inevitably the engine was brought back to the shed and disposed of, and during an eight-hour shift this tedious performance might be repeated three times. Although a driver and fireman were booked together as in any other link, there was no guarantee that they would always work as a team. For example, if a driver was selected for a job because of his specialised route knowledge and his fireman had not arrived for some reason, then the next available fireman would be borrowed. Absenteeism was not at all uncommon amongst the unmarried firemen, but because there was such an acute shortage of men the management were forced to be unusually tolerant.

Just to keep one's eye in and interest alive, so to speak, there were fortunately a few road jobs thrown in, which took one to such relatively faraway places as Bromsgrove or even Gloucester in the west, or Burton, Derby and Leicester in the north and east. However, such was the volume of traffic in those days that even with local turns a fair amount of overtime could be had and one was always asked if one wished to work on Sunday if normal booked times allowed. My mate Harold, having three children, could never take home too much money, and as I now had a motorcycle to pay off I was also quite happy to earn a bit extra. We therefore always asked for any sort of work on a Sunday for which we were, of course, paid double time. Frequently these Sunday jobs took the form of ballast trains, since track maintenance was carried out between midnight Saturday and midnight Sunday. They were not very exacting from the firing point of view, but like shunting duties demanded continual vigilance and attention when movements were being made. To relieve my boredom, Harold

usually allowed me to occupy the driver's side, a
privilege I gratefully accepted.

One Sunday, however, we were told to book on for a
special coal train which was to be moved from Water
Orton to the Corporation sidings at Washwood Heath,
destined for the power station at Nechells, which we
gathered was rather low on stocks. Things were more
than usually chaotic that day, because a new crossover
was being installed at Washwood Heath Junction and
traffic was being kept to an absolute minimum - even
passenger trains were being diverted where possible.
We booked on at 6.00 a.m., prepared Class 8F 8669, rang
off the shed at 7.15 and proceeded tender-first to Water
Orton with our guard in attendance on the footplate.
Our passage to Water Orton was in itself unusual, since
to avoid the work at Washwood Heath Junction we were
diverted over the up sidings and then allowed to run
through an empty road, set aside there for the purpose,
until we came out at Bromford. From there we travelled
to our destination on the up main. At Water Orton we
discovered just how special our train was to be. Apparently it consisted of two coal trains which had been
left there overnight, and we were to couple these
together and haul the combined load, which totalled no
less than 105 wagons equal to 116. This was in round
figures something in excess of 1,500 tons. My first
question to Harold was, 'Will she do it?' 'Don't know,'
he replied. 'I've never had that many on before, but
we'll soon find out.' We had, of course, to first draw
half the train out, and then set back on the remainder
before all was coupled up and we were ready to go. Our
guard gave us the signal and started walking back to
his distant brake, while Harold eased open the regulator.

We felt the pull of the heavy wagons as the couplings
stretched out and, as we tended to be dragged to a
standstill, Harold compensated by progressively opening
the regulator. Despite a full head of steam and the
gear lever at maximum cut-off, we were soon on full
first valve as we wumphed majestically out on the down
main. The rail was dry and 8669 gave not the slightest
hint of a slip as I watched the incredible line of
wagons slowly worm out of the sidings. However, such
was its length that even my eagle eyesight was not up
to being able to see that our guard had climbed safely
aboard, over seven hundred yards back. We therefore
assumed all was well and, winding the reversing screw

back to 60 per cent cut-off, Harold heaved the regulator
up to the horizontal. Gradually our blast took on a
crisper note and 8669 began to show her mettle by gradually accelerating that gargantuan load up the 1 in 975
gradient from Water Orton. Her task was made no easier
by the fact that many of the wagons were equipped with
the old greasebox type axle bearings which dragged
heavily until warmed up.

As our speed increased, so the exhaust acquired that
gunfire-like thump typical of Black Fives and 8Fs when
working hard, and I revelled in the exhilaration of this
unusual feat. I was carrying a medium-sized fire, but
with this treatment I soon had to start shovelling in
earnest. By now, however, I had gained sufficient
experience with 8Fs to be able to cope reasonably well
and, having recently perfected the technique of bouncing
the shovel blade on the mouthpiece ring, I could not
only reach the front of the box but I could place each
shovelful in roughly the desired spot. I found that by
building the fire up level with the mouthpiece, the rear
half of the grate could be fired with the minimum of
effort by more or less rolling the coal in to the
required area. Using only the rear damper caused more
rapid combustion in this section that was easiest to
reach and, together with the natural tendency for coal
to shake forward, meant that one could normally fire two
shovelsful to the rear half to only one at the front.

Harold did not allow our speed to build up too high,
because stopping a 1,500-ton train with only the engine
brake had to be considered; consequently, he came back
to the first valve and further reduced the cut-off when
we approached the distant for Castle Bromwich. We still
had a clear road, though, and Harold opened out once
more as the gradient stiffened to 1 in 486. Eventually
we were brought to a halt at Bromford Bridge home
signal, where we learned just how much energy is stored
up in a 1,500-ton train, even running at only 15m.p.h.
On drawing up to the signal box, the bobby informed us
that a traffic inspector was waiting at Washwood Heath
Junction to see us over the permanent way works and to
supervise our rather complicated and unorthodox entry
into the Corporation sidings.

Getting away again on the 1 in 326 gradient did
provoke a slip, but 8669 kept her feet very well as we
struggled slowly towards the junction, until we were
stopped by a hand signalman protecting the maintenance
operations. Harold decided to walk the two hundred

yards to the box in order to ascertain just what procedures had been worked out for us, leaving me in charge
with the instructions to bring her up when they were
ready. Some minutes later he reappeared in the distance
with a tall gentleman wearing a felt hat, who I
concluded was the traffic inspector. After some
whistle-blowing and waving of arms, the hand signalman
indicated that it was all clear to proceed, so I gave a
toot of acknowledgment and released the hand brake.
Being still on a gradient of 1 in 326, the couplings
were at full stretch but despite the great weight
dragging on the drawbar, 8669 shuddered into motion as
soon as I hauled the regulator up on full first valve.
After a few yards, by way of experiment, I wound the
reversing screw back to give 45 per cent cut-off and
then quickly heaved the regulator wide open. At this
setting she moved forward very smoothly, pulling her
great load at a steady walking pace towards where
Harold and the inspector were standing engrossed in
conversation. It was the one and only time I ever had
the good fortune to handle a train of over 1,000 tons,
albeit for just about one furlong, but it went down in
my diary as a personal all-time record which is now not
likely to be broken. I dropped back to the first valve
just before they climbed aboard and, with Harold once
again at the controls, we chugged slowly over the
unballasted crossover at the permitted 5m.p.h., giving
the sweating workmen there quite a substantial breather.
It was arranged that we drew ahead of Washwood Heath
Number One signal box and then backed across the road
to enter the Corporation sidings via Hill 60, but such
was the length of our train that the inspector alighted
by Saltley station to relay the necessary signals to
us. Eventually the operation was accomplished, but it
is worth recording that it required full gear and a
wide open regulator to push that huge load back over
Hill 60's hump.
    As the weeks passed by we did manage the odd job
which took us further afield, and on two consecutive
days we ran a Class A to Burton with a 4F and a Class B
to Bromsgrove with a faithful old 3F. The former trip
was interesting but uneventful, except that I had
difficulty in maintaining steam, but the latter stands
out in my mind because it was my first look at the
formidable Lickey incline. Our train was a mixed
freight of 38 wagons which, although a fair load for a
3F, did not prove too troublesome on the long haul of

mainly adverse gradients up from Duddeston Road to Barnt
Green. From here we turned into the down loop at Blackwell, where we stood for an hour or so alongside the
golf course. I had heard many exciting tales of various
exploits on the bank and was all agog to see what it was
like. Now here it lay at last, just round the next bend
while we were cooped up waiting for all the morning
passenger trains to clear the line. Just when I felt
that I could stand the waiting no longer, the signal
came off, we eased out on to the main line and trundled
slowly through the station.

A grey-haired rotund figure dressed in a shunter's
uniform called a cheery good morning to us as he walked
in a rolling gait along the platform, swinging in his
right hand a rather battered brake-stick. A brake-
stick, incidentally, is a piece of stout hardwood about
the size of a baseball bat but, while the top half or
handle is round, the bottom half is of square section.
Its function is for gaining extra purchase when pinning
down brake handles of wagons by the simple expedient of
inserting the end of the stick between the brake handle
and the solebar of the wagon, and then using it as a
lever. A hefty brakeman or guard, by swinging on the
end of the brake-stick in this manner, can in fact even
lock the wheels, providing that the brake mechanism is
in good condition.

Just beyond the end of the platform I noticed an
ancient black hut and a prominent signboard stating that
all goods trains were to stop in order to pin down
brakes, and here we ground to a halt. The brakeman
walked back to the guard, with whom he consulted with
regard to the load of the train. Having come to agree-
ment as to the number of wagons to have their brakes
applied which might be, say, one in three, they then
walked forwards towards the engine, dropping the brake
handles from their resting places as appropriate but not
pinning them down, the guard taking the up side while
the brakeman attended to the down or platform side. On
arrival back at the engine they would give us the tip to
proceed, and we would draw slowly ahead on to the
incline proper, while both men pinned down the brakes
with the aid of their sticks as the wagons came by them.
This technique required a high degree of skill from the
driver and a considerable amount of dexterity from both
guard and brakeman, since if we went too fast they would
not be able to pin down the brakes properly, and a runaway would be inevitable. On the other hand, if we went

too slowly we might be dragged to a standstill, in which
case some of the brakes would have to be picked up again
and as often as not this would again result in a
runaway. The driver had to play it very much by feel
and instinct, for every train and engine was different.
It was, in fact, an open secret that every honest driver
freely admitted that, once over the top, one could never
guarantee being able to stop at the bottom.

While waiting for the guard to return, I was able to
take a good long look at this famous Lickey incline.
Visibility was well-nigh perfect as I peered down that
fantastic two-and-a-quarter mile stretch of perfectly
straight track inclined at 1 in 37. It was almost like
looking down from the top of an Alpine ski jump, and
even the dimmest of intellects could well imagine the
sort of speeds one would be achieving if allowed to run
free right to the bottom. I had run the fire down quite
considerably during our idle period in the loop and,
being already on a falling gradient of 1 in 291, had not
bothered to put any more on, so I was somewhat surprised
when Harold, after a quick glance into the firebox,
advised me to spread a few shovels of coal around the
grate. 'We often have to work quite hard to drag the
train over the top when the brakes have been dropped,'
he explained, 'and if we knock the steam pressure down
too much we will be short of brake power.' I had just
finished when our guard shouted to us that all was ready
and we could draw ahead. After releasing the hand
brake, Harold gently opened the regulator in order to
stretch out the couplings and then, as the drag of the
dropped brakes was felt, he fed in more power to try and
keep our speed at a steady walking pace. It was of
course very difficult, because as more of the train got
on the 1 in 37 incline it tended to accelerate, and as
we accelerated both guard and brakeman pinned the brakes
down harder. Therefore a constant surging was at first
noticeable and Harold had to make continual adjustments
to the regulator. With half the train on the incline
we were virtually on full first valve and it was more
like going up bank than down; then suddenly we began
to run more easily and Harold shut back to just a breath
of steam. The transition was quite remarkable, and I
quickly realised that the force of gravity was now
taking over. Closing the regulator, Harold immediately
started to apply the steam brake while at the same time
shouting for me to wind the hand brake on as hard as I
could get it. We were now travelling at about 10m.p.h.

and it occurred to me that if we went much faster, the
guard might be hard put to rejoin his brake van. As if
reading my thoughts, Harold called over his shoulder.
'See if you can spot the guard, mate, he should signal
on your side.' I leaned out of the uprights, staring
intently towards the rear of the train, which now
appeared to have passed the brakeman's hut. The background was dark but there, waving from the side of the
van, was a piece of newspaper - attached, I assumed, to
our guard via an unseen arm.

Harold was applying the brake intermittently,
initially holding it on for five or ten seconds and then
releasing it for a similar period, so that our speed
remained reasonably constant at some 15m.p.h. Then I
noticed that the periods of application began to exceed
those of release, while at the same time our pace,
instead of being checked, was inexorably increasing.
By now the distant signals for Bromsgrove could be
clearly seen, and with the left one off we were to be
diverted on to the slow line at Bromsgrove station. A
ten-coach express hauled by a Black Five, and pushed
energetically by Big Emma, the 0-10-0 bank engine,
blasted past on the up, adding a false impression of
speed to our descent. Or was it false, because Harold
now had the brake on continuously and without doubt we
were going faster than before. Seeing my enquiring
look, Harold smiled resignedly. 'Well, that's it, old
son. The train's in charge now; we can't do much more
except put the sanders on and pull her into reverse, but
we are going to run well past now, so it's not worth
straining the mechanism. In fact,' he continued while
turning off the small ejector which was no longer of any
use, 'if you haven't got control of the train by the
time you reach the back 'uns for Bromsgrove, you can be
sure of running away. I wish I had as many pounds as
times I've run past the column,' he sighed pensively,
'but there's nothing to worry about, really. We'll get
a bit of kick on the crossover, but it's the finest
pair of facing points in the country, and we're bound to
stop somewhere, so sit down and enjoy the ride.'

Enjoy it I did - my most exciting experience yet, and
I relished every second, hopping from one side of the
footplate to the other, first looking forward to judge
how far we yet had to travel and then looking back at
the trail of smoke and dust pouring up from the train
wheels. Our own brake blocks were now getting pretty
warm and the smell of hot metal and burning oil was

strong in the cab. By leaning well out I could clearly
see the catherine wheel-like showers of sparks splashing
along the whole length of our underframes.

The base of the 1 in 37 ends at Bromsgrove station,
where it eases for a short distance to 1 in 186 before
dropping at 1 in 105 to the water column, relief cabin
and signal box at Bromsgrove South. We were travelling
at something like 40m.p.h. when we passed with surprising smoothness through the crossover at the beginning of
the station platform and, still being on a falling
gradient, our speed did not noticeably diminish until
passing the water column we had intended to stop at.
Then with unexpected rapidity our pace fell when the
whole train was on the 1 in 283 section between the
South box and Stoke Works Junction, which was half a
mile farther on. Even so, when we eventually pulled up
with a jerk amid the shriek of tortured brakes, we had
run by several train lengths. Harold explained that it
was impossible to move until the pinned-down brakes had
been lifted; even if one had only run past a couple of
wagon lengths, the same procedure had to be adopted. He
therefore took the coal pick and started walking back
towards the guard, unpinning the wagon brakes. Not
without some considerable effort did we set back to the
column, where we were relieved by a Worcester crew who
seemed well pleased over the extra delay. Sadly, we
were sent home in the brake van of a northbound fitted,
since there was not another train available for us to
work back with, so I was therefore denied the experience
of firing up Lickey.

Although it was now the height of the summer season
and special passenger trains were thick on the ground,
they always seemed to elude us. This was in part due to
the fact that Harold did not sign for places beyond
Gloucester and Derby, and most of these specials
required working to Bristol or Sheffield. However, one
Saturday morning I walked into the lobby at 9.00 a.m. to
find that my arrival was greeted with a certain amount
of relief by the foreman's clerk. It appeared that my
old friend Doug Pinkerton was booked to relieve a special passenger train at Saltley station that had
originated from Sheffield, and work it forward to Bath.
Unfortunately his mate had been taken sick and I was
the most eligible fireman to fill the vacancy. 'Do you
feel fit enough to tackle it then?' hailed Doug in his
usual hearty manner after the situation had been
explained to me. 'You bet I do,' I replied

enthusiastically as I hastily booked on. 'Tell me,
though, why do we have to relieve it at Saltley station
and not New Street?' 'Because it's booked through non-
stop, so we're taking it up Camp Hill bank. In fact,
the only stop we will have to make is for water at
Gloucester station,' he replied, already moving towards
the lobby doorway. 'Come on, we're due to relieve them
at 9.28 a.m., so we haven't got much time.'

My head was in a bit of a whirl at the speed at which
events were now happening, for I had had no time to
prepare myself mentally for this situation. I learned
from Doug, as he headed for Saltley station at his usual
half gallop, that in summer passenger specials bound for
the west were frequently routed via Camp Hill, thus
avoiding the congestion of New Street. Likewise, empty
stock specials working up from the west with their
mammoth twenty-coach trains also used this convenient
avoiding line. We arrived on the platform with a few
minutes to spare, but 9.28 a.m. came and went without
any sign of our train. In fact, the slow that should
have followed on behind arrived first, but as soon as it
had departed jauntily on its way to New Street, our
special hove into view. It was moving quite slowly, and
glided to a smooth halt at the end of the platform
opposite to where we were standing. It was exactly
9.42 a.m., fourteen minutes late - not a good start to
the trip - but Bath was a long way off, and a lot could
happen in two hours or so. The engine was one of our
own Saltley Black Fives, 4804, and although its appearance was drab and grimy it looked pretty good to me.
The fact that people with their heads poking out of the
windows were watching us made me feel pretty proud as I
stepped on the footplate, but my attention was
concentrated on the Sheffield crew we were relieving.

The fireman was a big lad, but he looked very hot and
a trifle distressed. 'Coils good, but 'appen there's
t'oil int' fire,' he said in about the broadest Yorkshire dialect I had ever heard. 'She's not steaming
well, but perhaps th'll manage. She's one o'thine.'
While I was trying to work out what he had said, I
overheard the Sheffield driver advise Doug that we had
on ten coaches, equal to about 320 tons. With that
information imparted, they climbed onto the platform
and, having stowed my gear, I quickly conducted a check
of the boiler pressure, water gauge and fire. She was
only showing 200lbs. per sq.in. on the clock and the
boiler was no more than two-thirds full, but she was

carrying a big fire in the rear half of the box,
although a little thin at the front end. Without further ado, I slammed about ten shovelsful in while Doug set
about the business of getting underway. We only had the
home signal off, so we eased gently out of the station
towards Duddeston Road where a train was crossing our
path on the up Camp Hill. Taking advantage of this
delay, I fired a further ten shovels of coal round the
box and was pleased to see a uniform grey column of
smoke coming from the chimney. I was also relieved to
see that the needle was steadily moving towards the red
line even with the injector on. As the Sheffield man
had stated, the coal was good, although some of the
lumps were more than king-size and would require breaking up. This may have contributed to the rather messy
state of the footplate. Having already developed a
fetish for tidiness, I hastened to clean up with hand
brush and slaking pipe while I had the chance. I found
the pipe was only half the normal length and, having no
nozzle, delivered a widely divergent spluttering spray
instead of the normal powerful jet. It was, however, to
prove a distinct advantage later in the day. Doug
meanwhile had crept up to Duddeston Road, and I was
leaning over the door behind him when I saw both home
and distant signals for the down Camp Hill come off
together.

The boiler had rallied nicely during the last few
minutes, the water was just in sight at the top of the
glass and pressure was now up to 220lbs per sq.in. - as
good as I could have wished for. Doug was in a determined mood, for as soon as we were safely over the
crossing he pulled the regulator over to full first
valve and only wound the reversing screw back a turn or
so. We had a fair load to hump up this bank unassisted
and Doug wanted to take a good run at it. Despite the
adverse 1 in 105, acceleration was impressive and of a
completely different order to that of any goods train.
The exhaust soon acquired a delightfully vicious bark
which caused, as we passed the loco, a number of heads
to be raised, along with the odd wave from colleagues we
knew. With all the distants off as far as we could see,
Doug heaved the regulator right across in preparation
for the 1 in 62 section up to St.Andrews, and at
55 per cent cut-off it was real stirring stuff as we
thundered up through the cutting without slackening
speed. I was, however, somewhat disconcerted by a
violent knock coming right up through the floorboards

at every revolution of the wheels; obviously 4804 was
not in mint condition. After passing Bordesley Junction
I started firing in earnest, although even prior to
this I had not been idle, since a number of large lumps
of coal required breaking up. With the firedoors open
about three inches, the exhaust colour was about ideal
but, even so, I was a trifle disappointed to find that,
despite having mortgaged the boiler level to the extent
that it was now showing two-thirds full, steam pressure
had also fallen to 215. With the fire in such obviously
good shape I had been led to suppose that a Black Five
should steam better than this. As the gradient eased to
1 in 280 at Camp Hill and our pace quickened noticeably,
Doug shortened the cut-off, for he was a great believer
in expansive working, but the knocking became so bad
that he quickly dropped it down a couple of turns and
reverted to the first valve. Even so, acceleration
continued as we passed Brighton Road, but now the cab
was rattling and clanging in sympathy with the big end
knock, and she was developing a violent intermittent
lateral shake which tended to throw me off balance,
particularly when I was firing - which required one foot
on the tender and one foot on the engine. I was getting
a little worried by the marked fall in steam pressure,
for the act of putting on the injector to maintain the
two-thirds boiler level had caused it to drop back to
under 200lbs. per sq.in.

Despite this, we stormed through Moseley Tunnel in
grand style and in seemingly no time at all we were
clattering through Kings Heath station. Here the gradient eased considerably to 1 in 1547 and Doug was able
to make further reductions in both regulator opening and
cut-off, but with the water now showing only half a
glass I was obliged to keep the injector on. This
caused the needle to drop back to 190lbs. per sq.in.
However, we were now on the one-mile level stretch
through Hazelwell and 4804 was rattling along at a fair
old pace. Through Lifford the gradient increased to
1 in 524, followed by a stretch of 1 in 301 up to Kings
Norton Junction, but the severe curves here and the
junction with the New Street line imposed a speed limit
of 25m.p.h., so Doug was therefore able to shut off
while still some distance away. I was glad of the brief
respite, but quite amazed by how quickly the boiler
recovered when the regulator was closed, so that by the
time Doug opened up again on the rise through Kings
Norton station the water was up to two-thirds and

steam pressure at 215lbs. per sq.in.

For the next three miles I knew we would be going up a ruling gradient of 1 in 301 to just beyond Cofton, so I was shovelling in coal on the little and often principle almost continuously while Doug seemed just as determined to remove it at approximately the same rate. Past Cofton the gradient was with us at 1 in 297 for half a mile before climbing once again up to the summit of Barnt Green. As our speed rose into the sixties at the bottom of this dip, the ferocious knocking, banging, swaying, rattling clamour on the footplate increased to unbearable proportions; even the cab itself was shaking like a jelly. Such was the vibration that the dampers would not stay open and I was obliged to prop up the rear one with a spanner. Doug was also suffering from vibration problems, or rather the regulator was, for being only partially open on the first valve the handle kept shaking itself shut. However, Doug had experienced this problem before and pulled from his pocket a small wedge-shaped block of wood which, when inserted against the quadrant stop, kept the regulator at something like three-quarters of the first valve. I later found that many drivers carried such wedges, since due to the differential action of the regulator when opening and closing this same piece of wood could also retain it on a fair amount of second valve. This was achieved by fully opening the regulator and then slowly closing it against the wedge; the second valve was still open, and in this condition was said to be gagged. If no wooden wedge was available, a small piece of coal served the same purpose, although of course this was inclined to break up in time.

To make life more intolerable for us, coal dust was swirling in from the tender, caught in the back draught, and with the built-in sprayer inoperative and an inadequate slaking pipe I could do little about it. This coal dust storm was being ably supplemented by a veritable hurricane of ash, borne in a stream of hot air coming up the gap between the boiler front and the footboards. Already I was soaked in perspiration and now the dust and grit was working its irritating way into every crevice of my clothing. If this was passenger work, I thought, as I staggered to regain my balance for the umpteenth time, you can stick it!

On the five-mile haul up to Barnt Green I had been forced to mortgage the boiler once more but, knowing that we would soon be descending at 1 in 37, I dare not

let it drop below the halfway mark, so by the time Doug
closed the regulator as we neared Blackwell pressure had
fallen to no more than 165lbs. per sq.in. Once over the
top and hurtling down the incline proper, Doug came over
and inspected the fire. 'What the devil's the matter
with the old camel?' he bellowed, as I quaffed down
mouthfuls of delicious cold water in an effort to quench
the raging thirst I had acquired. 'Seems O.K.,' he
remarked, a puzzled frown creasing his forehead but,
seeing that I was more than somewhat overheated, quickly
fired a dozen shovels of coal round the box.

Determined to get some time back if possible, Doug
allowed the train to coast unchecked for quite some
distance and we descended like a plunging meteor. With
steam off, she was much more smooth and quiet, and for
the first time I was able to really enjoy our speed. As
before with the regulator shut, recovery was remarkably
quick, the needle fairly leaping round the clock in spite
of the injector being on continuously. Nearing the
bottom, Doug was concentrating on some pretty heavy brake
applications, but at the same time he was fully aware of
the state of the boiler. 'I reckon I know what's wrong
with her,' he suddenly shouted. 'A pound to a penny some
of the superheater elements are blowing. That would
also account for us using so much water.' I was insuf-
ficiently experienced to be able to offer an opinion, but
from the high regard that everyone seemed to have of
Black Fives they must as a whole be an awful lot better
than this one.

It was just as well that we ran through Bromsgrove
station on the fast line, for our speed seemed rather
higher than the permitted 40m.p.h., and with the gradient
with us at 1 in 283 we were soon thrashing along again in
a pandemonium of ear-shattering din. I had just staggered across to Doug in order to verify that we were
passing Stoke Works Junction when, with a loud bang, my
gauge glass burst. The cab was immediately filled with
steam but without thinking I grasped the combined
shut-off cocks and tugged them down. I had often
wondered in the past how I would react to such a situation, and I was pleased to find that I had acted on
reflex without worrying about the possibility of being
scalded - such was the trust I placed in wearing leather
gloves. I now had no knowledge at all of the road ahead,
but Doug had previously advised me that the gradients in
general were mainly in our favour - with the needle
backsliding once more, however, I started firing in

earnest. With our speed in the seventies I would dearly
have liked to sit down and watch the scenery flash by,
but since sitting was impossible - Doug had long since
taken to standing - and with coal to be got forward and
broken up between bouts of almost continual shovelling,
quite apart from juggling with the injector, I was
constantly occupied. It was also infernally hot in the
cab, and I soon found myself staggering to the side
window for a few seconds every minute or so to gasp in
great gulps of air which, although warm, seemed delightfully cold by comparison. Were it not for this manmade
gale, I would have expired long ago.

Despite my all-out efforts, which Doug kindly
supplemented with bouts of firing when I was occupied in
the tender with the coal pick, we rarely saw more than
180lbs. per sq.in. on the clock and when the water level
fell below half a glass, Doug would shut off for a short
period to rally the boiler. That it did so with extreme
rapidity certainly gave credence to his theory that the
superheater elements were leaking, but for all her ails
we certainly seemed to be eating up the miles at a crazy
pace. The terrible racket and roughness made it seem
faster, of course, but I had no time at all to count the
seconds between mileposts. Occasionally when gasping at
the side window I noted such meaningless names as
Spetchley, Pirton and Defford, and after the latter Doug
yelled that from here down to Eckington was about the
fastest section of the run. It felt like it, too, for
we seemed to be making contact with the rails only every
hundred yards or so. Soon we were through Aschurch and
thrashing on towards Cheltenham, the period of coasting
having enabled me to fill the boiler, but our steam
pressure was no more than 190lbs. per sq.in. As can be
imagined, it was getting harder than ever to fire due
to the continual need to go into the tender and shovel
coal forward, a task rendered difficult by the wild
oscillations and unpleasant by the blizzard of coal
dust whirling round its interior. Contrary to enginemen's normal desires, I was very thankful indeed when
we were severely checked by signals at Cheltenham.
Once more the respite was just long enough to recover
both steam pressure and water levels to a respectable
amount, ready for the dash down to Gloucester. Doug
consulted his watch as we approached the sharply curved
platform. 'We've pulled back five minutes, mate,' he
announced cheerfully, and with the road now clear he
heaved open the regulator to such effect that he caused

many of the passengers waiting on the platform to
scuttle quickly back from the edge. Having gained time
despite our difficulties, Doug was inspired to even
greater efforts over the six-mile stretch to Gloucester
and, since for the first time in miles we were showing
225lbs. per sq.in. on the clock, he felt justified in
letting rip to some purpose. As for myself, I realised
that my blood sugar was beginning to run out and my
limbs were beginning to shake with the sustained effort
as we hurtled through Churchdown station in a leaping,
clanging fury of sound and motion. I hated to admit it
to myself, but I knew that I had just about shot my
bolt.

Approaching Gloucester the Great Western tracks ran
parallel to our own for a stretch and, forgetting our
tiredness for a few moments, we were able to enjoy the
boyish pleasure of steadily overhauling one of their
expresses. Then with the water level perilously low and
pressure back to 170lbs. per sq.in., we shut off to
coast to a halt dead on target for the water column at
the end of the platform. I climbed wearily on top of
the tender and with my remaining strength pulled the
heavy bag into position. We had cut it very fine
indeed, for there was barely any in the bottom of the
tank. While taking on water, I dragged myself back onto
the footplate in order to make use of a static and
stable platform to fire the front half of the grate,
which had become sadly neglected over the last mile or
two. Gratefully I allowed Doug to take over the shovel
while I pulled more of our now much-depleted coal supply
forward.

The remainder of the trip to Bath was nothing short
of a nightmare for me; my whole body became numb with
fatigue, and I was staggering about my tasks like a
zombie. Were it not for Doug firing the front end we
would never have made it. As it was, I realised that
even six months ago I would not have had the strength
and stamina to continue as far as this. I was driving
myself beyond my normal physical limits by sheer will-
power, spurred on partly by determination and partly by
the fear that if I let Doug down now, I would not be
taken on any good jobs again. In my daze I was half
consciously aware of passing through Wickwar Tunnel, and
of places like Yate, Westerleigh and Mangotsfield,
praying all the time that my torment would soon be over.
I dragged the firedoors open yet again wondering whether
I could find the necessary strength to pick up the

shovel, let alone use it, when Doug laid a restraining
hand on my shoulder. 'Run it down now,' he bellowed in
my ear. 'We're very nearly there and I'll be shutting
off in a minute.' Thank God for that, I thought, as I
put my head in the slipstream for a moment in an effort
to cool my superheated brow. Once more, however, pride
overcame my exhaustion and I quickly scrambled around
the shaking and bucking footplate, sweeping up coal
spillage and dust before giving a final swill down with
the slaking pipe. Doug had shut off before I had
finished, but even so I was able to sit down for the
first time in what seemed hours and enjoy the approach
into Bath. In the brilliant sunshine it looked like
heaven for more reasons than one, and I was most
impressed by the wonderful cleanliness of the buildings,
which contrasted very favourably with Saltley's
unattractive grime.

We came to a halt in Bath station exactly seven
minutes late, a wonderful tribute to Doug's determination, superb enginemanship and his intimate knowledge
of the road. To have accomplished the recovery of
seven minutes with a defective and rough engine plus a
young and relatively inexperienced fireman was a fine
achievement. Quite a number of drivers I came to know
in the future would have called it a day and failed the
engine at Gloucester for any one of the above reasons.

I was already feeling a sight better when we were
uncoupled by the station staff and sent off to Bath
loco. On arrival there we were supposed to hand over
to a Bath crew who had been detailed to clean the fire
and get her ready again for our return working of a
special relief train. This was due to depart at
2.40 p.m., calling at Gloucester, Cheltenham and New
Street, where we were to be relieved. They were
waiting for us as we came to a halt, but when the
driver saw our appearance and the virtually empty
tender he cocked an enquiring eye at Doug and said,
'Had a rough trip, brother?' 'Like hell we have,'
retorted Doug. 'Don't touch her yet,' he continued.
'I want the fitters to have a look at the elements.
I reckon they're blowing badly.' 'Well, you've certainly used some coal,' mused the Bath driver as if
mentally calculating how many tubs would be required to
fill it, for they had no mechanical plant here.

The fitters subsequently carried out their
inspection while I was busily engaged in trying to
drink the local reservoir dry. In a nutshell, it

turned out that three superheater elements were blowing
to such an extent that it was a wonder we got there at
all. They could do nothing in the time available and,
unless Doug was prepared to take her back as she was,
another engine would have to be found. Suitable spare
engines were hard to come by on a busy summer Saturday
and I had the pleasant thought that we might get a
Southern West Country Pacific, since a number were
standing in the shed yard. At first, the foreman said
he had only a Class 4F 0-6-0 available, but when Doug
told him in no uncertain terms just what he could do
with this, he went off to consult with Control. We were
in the mess room, having just consumed a well-earned
lunch, when he joined us with the news that we were to
take 5265, another Saltley Black Five which had been
prepared for a later job and for which another substitute had now been found. Doug seemed well pleased, for
he turned to me with a grin and said, 'That's O.K.,
mate. She's a good 'un. I had her only a few days ago
on a job to Sheffield.'

Whilst not in exactly pristine condition externally,
there was certainly nothing wrong with 5265 mechanically
for, although we were some four minutes late departing
from Bath, again with a ten-coach train, Doug had more
than made this up by the time we arrived at Gloucester.
With her, there were no excessive knocks or rattles and,
though admittedly I was kept very busy, every pound of
steam generated was used in the cylinders, not wasted up
the chimney. Pressure never dropped below 200, nor the
water level below three-quarters of a glass; moreover,
apart from not having to fire her so heavily, the coal
was available right there on the shovelling plate, so I
always had a few minutes to recover between bouts of
firing. Nevertheless, I was glad enough to hand over to
my relief at New Street, and travelling back to Saltley
by bus I suddenly felt strangely tired. The heat, noise
and abnormal sustained effort had all contributed and,
now that I had at last relaxed, I began to feel their
combined effect. My ears were still full of the frantic
clamour of the footplate and my head was still swimming
with the fast-moving events of the day as I walked
across to the cycle sheds. Exhausted, yes, but I was
well satisfied with my first taste of passenger work.
Once bitten by this passenger bug, I hankered for more
and whether it was a case of now being regarded as a
safe risk or whether it was just the luck of the draw I
do not know, but before the summer season drew to a

close I managed to enjoy a few more such turns.

These included a Blackpool special, which I worked as
far as Crewe, and a run to Gloucester with Harold which
proved nearly as hectic as the one with 4804. Again we
had a Black Five which, although the boiler was sound,
was mechanically very rough, but the main problem this
time stemmed from the fact that it had been coaled with
about 80 per cent slack. Consequently I never stopped
shovelling and rarely did we see more than 200lbs. per
sq.in. on the gauge. All in all, though, I enjoyed the
speed and excitement these jobs provided and the experience gained by having to fire up to two hours
continuously. It was, therefore, something of a
let-down when September arrived and we found ourselves
back with the routine of local relief and few prospects
of reasonable road jobs. Furthermore I was beginning
to feel a little unsettled around this period, since I
had been required to register for National Service after
my eighteenth birthday in August, and consequently I
expected my call-up papers to arrive with every post.

The Control link formed the only pool from which
firemen could be readily drawn to cover any unforeseen
emergency, and I therefore found myself with several
different drivers on as many different jobs in the
course of a single week. While this had the advantage
of broadening my experience at a faster pace than
normal, it also meant that I never had time to get to
know the ways of my driver or the job concerned. On
many occasions I was literally groping in the dark
without sufficient general knowledge and skill to execute my work as competently as I would have desired.
The manpower shortage naturally caused an excessive
amount of overtime to be worked and it was not unusual
to relieve a westbound train at Water Orton or Castle
Bromwich, and be relieved twelve hours later without
still having reached Washwood Heath.

As the autumn nights lengthened, life developed into
a humdrum seven-day week of bed and work with often
precious little of the former, and many weeks passed
when I rarely saw the light of day. All this activity
tended to produce fatigue and a dulling of the intel-
lect in both drivers and fireman alike, so that when
standing on a bleak and exposed section of track for
interminable hours conversation lapsed, and the ability
to snatch a quick forty winks took top priority. Not
that this was always possible, for with the exception

of Class 3F and 4F 0-6-0s most engines were not built for relaxation and, in any case, being soaked and frozen on one side while at the same time roasted on the other is not exactly conducive to sleep.

Looking back on that winter of 1951-52, it would be fair to say that it was the least happy and exciting period of my railway career. Based on the philosophy that the human brain endeavours to forget unpleasant experiences, it must have been so, for I remember less clearly the details of the individual workings of the latter half of my stay in the Control link than any other time. However, a marathon turn, again with Doug Pinkerton, who was never one to shy at overtime, stands out in my mind. One December night we worked a 'Maltese' (at least four fitted vehicles next to the engine) to Derby North. This in itself was a pleasant change from local relief work, but we had been badly delayed during the journey and had already completed seven hours by the time we relieved a Class B freight bound for Washwood Heath at Derby North cabin. Our trip home was the usual stop-and-go ritual until we were turned in at Elford, roughly halfway between Burton and our destination, in the early hours of the morning. Here we remained for no less than six hours without moving a wheel and standing at that exposed spot, wrong way to the weather on a freezing night, was an agony best forgotten. When eventually we did get the road we had been on duty over fifteen hours and the need for food and drink, both of which had long since run out, was getting more than somewhat pressing. Even then a clear path was not yet available and another two hours or more had elapsed by the time we were finally relieved at Washwood Heath Junction. Feeling a little the worse for wear, we walked to the shed and booked off exactly nineteen hours after signing on, which was for me to stand as an all-time record.

With the coming of spring our spirits lifted, and I found myself looking forward once again to the prospect of being able to work the numerous passenger specials which I now felt more competent to handle. After all, I had another year's experience and physical development behind me and it was logical to assume that this time I would get a rather thicker slice of the cake. Furthermore, it was now eight months since I had registered for National Service and, not having heard anything since, I was beginning to believe that they had forgotten all

about me. The uncertainty of the past had consequently
receded and I was fervently hoping to be booked with a
driver who, like Doug Pinkerton, had a very extensive
road card. Alas, it was not to be, for when the May
change-over lists were posted I found to my intense
surprise that I had been promoted, not to another mate
in the Control link or even to the next link, the
Specials, but right up into the Trip link with driver
J.Greatrex.

VII

THE TRIP LINK

After the variations, the long hours, the uncertainties and generally hurly-burly of the Control, I unexpectedly found myself in the relatively well-ordered tranquillity of the Trip link in the company of an equally well-ordered and tranquil mate.

It was around this time I noted one of Nature's unexplained mysteries. Over the age of about 45, drivers tended to follow one of two courses with regard to their physical appearances. Either they seemed hell-bent on adopting the rotund hogshead model or they took on the aspect of something resembling a bean pole.

My new mate Jack Greatrex fell into this latter, generally longer-living category. Jack, although only four years from retirement, was still blessed with finely chiselled features and undoubtedly must have been quite good-looking in his younger days. His temperament and demeanour was calm and quiet, but belonging as he did to the older school of ex-L.N.W.R. drivers, was set in his ways and quite a disciplinarian.

We first met in the lobby at 5.00 a.m. Monday morning prior to booking on for 28 Trip, a Bordesley job for which we prepared our own 8F before setting out for the day's work. I soon discovered that everything had to be exactly right in every meticulous detail, and if only working a local tripper he would not take the engine off the shed if it showed the slightest defect. Had he been preparing a Carlisle, he could not have been more thorough. This, of course, meant that I too had to work to his high standard, which was, I must admit, a welcome change to the often slack attitudes found in the common working of my previous link. For example, he insisted that the sanding gear was topped up and tested and that I spread a quantity of limestone over the grate before building up the fire. Furthermore, both injectors had to be proved satisfactory before moving on to the table and, although we would not be going within miles of the nearest water troughs, I had to operate the scoop while he inspected its action from beneath the tender. From the appearance of his somewhat faded but nevertheless well-pressed and immaculate overalls, I might have guessed that he was a stickler for cleanliness, so it was no surprise to find that all traces of coal and dirt had

to be quickly banished from the footplate. Moreover,
the tender had to be properly trimmed and the dust therein well and truly laid by a generous application of the
slaking pipe, for he expected to finish up the week with
overalls very little dirtier than when he started.
However, since this fitted in very nicely with my own
ideas on how a footplate should be kept, it proved no
hardship and in this respect we got on extremely well
from the word go.

Bearing these aspects of his character in mind, it
was therefore not unusual for us to book off the shed
late, and on this first Monday we were something like
twenty minutes awry when we finally departed. This
delay was brought about by the need to obtain the serv-
ices of a fitter and mate in order to attend to the
sanding gear and a slight blow on the small ejector.
When everything was in apple-pie order and we were
trundling sedately, tender-first, along the up goods
line heading for Washwood Heath Junction, I thought it
was about time I got to know something about the job and
I questioned Jack accordingly.

'I've never worked a Bordesley tripper properly,' I
said openly, since I wished to make this point quite
clear. 'Just relieved one or two and brought the engine
to the shed. What exactly do we do?' 'Oh, it's very
straightforward,' replied Jack in his quiet, precise
manner. 'We pick up a train at the junction or sometimes the West End, and work it into Bordesley. Then we
shunt it as required, run over to the down sidings,
collect another train from there and work it back over
Hill 60, and then start all over again. Nothing much to
it, really, but it involves a lot of waiting around,
particularly in Bordesley, where we have to have a good
clear path before crossing their main lines. The Great
Western get very upset if we stop one of their expresses
and, of course, we cut right across their up and down
fast and slow lines when drawing out of the down
sidings.' I was able to picture the scene fairly
clearly in my mind's eye, for I had studied this
expanse of tracks at Bordesley hundreds of times when
crossing over them on the Bank Pilots.

At Washwood Heath Number One signal box we whistled
three short, two short for the junction and continued
to clank easily down past the hump of Hill 60 to the
left. Stopping at the ground signal just beyond the
junction box we waited some minutes for a path, and I
took the opportunity to ask Jack about the other jobs

in the link. It seemed that we worked as far as Kingsbury to the north, to Rubery up the Halesowen branch in
the west, and to Aldridge over the Walsall line, while
at the same time covering most places on Midland metals
enclosed in this triangle. Not having yet visited any
of the venues mentioned I was about to question him
further when the signal dropped and we hastily crossed
over to the down sidings. Here, under the guidance of a
shunter, we backed on our train and waited for the
appearance of our guard. Jack, meanwhile, instructed me
to position our headlamps for trip working, which was
one lamp over the left buffer, and having done this I
packed some coal under the firedoors and into the back
corners. When ignorant of a job's routine, it was always
difficult to achieve the fine balance of just carrying
the correct amount of fire; only experience could teach
one that.

Shortly afterwards Dennis, our guard, climbed somewhat
laboriously on to the footplate in response to Jack's
invitation to partake of a quick cup of tea. Holding
the lid in one hand, he consulted a scrap of cardboard
torn from a cigarette packet (guards, I found, univers-
ally seemed to prefer such pieces of cardboard to
notebooks) and advised us that we had 48 wagons equal to
56 of mineral. To clarify this remark, I should explain
that for loading purposes a mineral wagon was calculated
at 13 tons, but when a number of 16-ton wagons was in a
train their extra weight had to be taken into consideration. In this instance we had 34 of the latter, which
meant that another 104 tons was being carried. Dividing
104 by 13 gives the equivalent additional number of
13-ton wagons which in this case was 8; therefore,
although we only had 48 wagons behind the tender, they
were equal in weight to 56 13-ton mineral wagons.

Having advised the yard staff that we were ready,
Dennis duly returned to his brake van, but a further
fifteen minutes elapsed before we were allowed to
proceed. With a load of over 900 tons behind the tender
we filtered out on to the down goods line and chugged
sedately up the 1 in 326 gradient towards the West End.
Being now somewhat familiar with an 8F's capabilities, I
decided to fire her lightly until we reached Duddeston
Road. At this time I was just developing the technique
of firing from the right side of the footplate and, like
most right-handed people, I found the action awkward and
unnatural, but since all modern engines were built to be
driven from the left side I felt I must practice as much

as possible until fully competent. Fortunately there is
room on an 8F to fire from either side, so initially I
tended to ring the changes, using the driver's side to
reach the front end only. Passing the pilot sidings I
had the pleasure of advising my old mate Bill that we
required his assistance to Bordesley and that I thought
his boiler front needed some attention, which needless
to say brought forth a not-unexpected rude gesture.

A long wait at Duddeston Road enabled Jack and me to
relate some of our respective background history to one
another, while at the same time it caused the usual
difficulty of trying to strike the balance of keeping
the fire reasonably lively without excessive blowing off.
Fortunately, the thermal reserve of an 8F's full boiler
was of great help, since one could virtually cover the
run to Bordesley without resorting to use of the injectors, but it was on these jobs that I learned to leave a
hole in the middle of the grate. By so doing, the fire
could be kept burning reasonably brightly with the back
damper open a couple of notches, while the air entering
via the hole prevented the firebox temperature from
reaching too high a level. When eventually we received
the right away, all I had to do was dig the firing
shovel blade into the live fire under the door and shoot
it down into the hole, when normal firing could then be
commenced immediately. This was the technique I used
now, so that by the time Jack had finished calling
attention to the fact that the signals were off by means
of the whistle, I had already filled in the hole, had
the firedoors closed and both rear damper and blower
wide open.

Getting our heavy train moving from a dead standstill
on the 1 in 105 gradient required full first regulator
and maximum cut-off, but as Bill also opened up and our
speed increased Jack was able to wind her up by degrees
to around 55 per cent. Even so, this was making a
pretty impressive volume of sound as we approached
Brickyard crossing but, despite the acceleration we had
achieved at this point, our speed rapidly fell away as
the gradient stiffened to 1 in 62. It was not Jack's
nature to rely too heavily on the pilot and he quickly
dropped her down to full gear once again for the stretch
up to the Coventry Road overbridge. Just beyond we
crossed over the facing points taking us on to the Great
Western and, by the time we passed Bordesley Junction
signal box, Jack had eased down to just a breath of
steam. 'We have to be careful here,' he explained.

'From climbing at 1 in 85 it suddenly dips down to the
stop signal at the entrance to the G.W. yard. If you
come over too fast the train can push you past the signal
and through the catch points.' I soon realised what he
meant, because Jack had to make two pretty hefty applications of the brake even though we were only travelling
at a walking pace before we eventually shuddered to a
halt at the signal. Some ten yards beyond this lay the
catch points he had referred to, and since the ground
here bore no trace of weeds, I gathered that someone had
been the victim of an embarrassing experience not too
long ago.

We waited at the signal for some twenty minutes
before the G.W. were ready for us. Bordesley is not a
very salubrious part of Birmingham and although we had a
fairly commanding view from the top of a thirty-foot
high embankment there was little of interest to see, so
we soon found ourselves talking shop. I quickly concluded that Jack was gently probing my knowledge of railway
working, my understanding of engines and whether I was
really interested in the job, without making it too
obvious. Having once established that I was keen to
learn more he adopted the role of tutor, and from then
onwards for the duration of my stay with him we had at
least one lesson per day on some aspect of railway life.
This might take the form of a question-and-answer
session about the function of locomotives or detailed
explanations of the rules and regulations and why they
were necessary. Jack also supported the theory that
firing was, or should be, a highly skilled art, and like
many other forms of physical endeavour expertise more
than made up for sheer brute strength. Whilst he was no
longer capable of practical demonstrations calling for
great effort, his counsel was always much appreciated.
However, I did consider his rather scornful regard of
ex-Midland firemen a little unfair because I found good
and bad firemen from all the pre-Grouping companies, but
his attitude was quite typical of many ex-L.N.W.R. men
who felt that even a navvy could fire the old Midland
engines.

Our interesting conversation was abruptly terminated
by a shrill blast on the G.W. head shunter's whistle
calling attention to the fact that the signal was now
off. We ran slowly into a lengthy siding, where for the
next twenty minutes we were required to do some energetic shunting. Despite its bulk, an 8F proved ideal for
shunting a heavy train, for it had the power to

accelerate smartly and, equally important, adequate
weight and brake power to stop again. The only drawback
was that it took a fair while and a lot of strenuous
winding to move the reversing screw from full forward
to full backward gear. Jack, never a husky chap and now
past his prime, was obviously happy when this unwelcomed
exercise finally came to a conclusion.

Another period of waiting followed before a path was
available for us to cross over to the down sidings.
Just before our signal dropped, I noticed one of our
Saltley 8Fs, hauling a moderate coal train, come off the
Bordesley Junction branch and without stopping head out
on to the up slow line, where it accelerated with
tremendous vigour in the direction of Small Heath.
Puzzled by the sight of a Saltley engine working on the
Western, I asked Jack what it was doing. 'Oh, that's
the Long Marston,' he replied. 'One of the Group One
jobs. They work a coal train up to Long Marston, which
is the other side of Stratford-upon-Avon, and then
return with a load of empties. It must have been Sam
Trayner. He's the only one in the link who works an
engine like that.' The name somehow rang a bell, and
then I remembered a very rough ride in a brake van back
from Water Orton one night when I had been working there
on the shunter. When in the brake van I had not appreciated his lack of finesse but at least as a spectator
I was forced to admire the determined way he handled
that mineral.

Having run briskly across to the down sidings, we
once more indulged in a period of shunting to make up
our train and when this was completed we settled down
to wait for another path. I recalled what Bill had
told me in the Bank Pilots about Bordesleys and it was
undoubtedly true that, from the fireman's point of view,
they were certainly not the most strenuous jobs at
Saltley. As far as I could see the main object to aim
for was to keep the fire as thin as possible and
thereby use the minimum amount of fuel. This would
then reduce the necessity to clean the fire and get
coal forward during the 24 hours the engine was in
service. A dozen shovelsful spread evenly round the
box sufficed for the quick gallop back to Bordesley
Junction, and thereafter it was merely a case of coasting down the bank to Hill 60. Here we followed the
regular procedure of pushing the preceding train over
the hump, and when this was done we shunted across the
road to Washwood Heath Junction and started all over

again. On average about two round trips would be
accomplished in an eight-hour shift but, as always, this
could vary according to prevailing conditions. The main
interest on these turns was the time available for disc-
ussion, and with a knowledgeable mate much could be
learned.
Although the routine followed a general pattern
boredom was kept at bay by day-to-day variations, one of
the welcome bonuses of railway work, and a new experience always seemed to turn up to add to one's store of
knowledge. On the Thursday this took the form of
sticking at St.Andrews, an event I had witnessed many
times from the rear end when on the pilots but never
from the train engine. After a prolonged dry spell,
steady drizzle had made the rails very slippery indeed,
and we unfortunately had an 8F which was long overdue
for a major shopping. She knocked and rattled in a most
disconcerting manner even at low speed and it was soon
apparent that the wheels were badly in need of new tyres.
On arrival at Washwood Heath Junction we found that
Dennis, our regular guard, had not turned up and that
his replacement was a pleasant young Pakistani whose
lack of experience was only matched by his peerless
enthusiasm. We later learned that he had not quite got
the hang of what loading tables were all about, and he
felt that it was his patriotic duty to couple just about
everything in the siding to our tender hook. Under
normal circumstances our all-up load would have been
limited to manageable proportions by the number of
vehicles we were allowed to take, but marshalled now to
the rear end of our fifty mineral wagons were two
special Weltags carrying a couple of outsize steel
ingots. These massive octagonal hunks of metal weighed
over eighty tons each, but in his innocence our guard
had regarded them as just two more mineral wagons. We
therefore set out with a train equivalent to over
seventy load of mineral, a fact soon made apparent by
the way we slipped and slithered up to the West End.
Jack had to use a fair amount of regulator and full gear
to move us up the 1 in 326 gradient and, because of the
slipping, he was forced to use the sanding gear almost
continuously. 'I'm sure our coloured friend has forgotten to take his brake off,' Jack muttered quietly in a
puzzled way as he juggled with the regulator in an
effort to keep us in motion. As far as we were
concerned we only had 52 wagons in tow, but it felt as
if we were still attached to the stop block.

Collecting our pilot en route we ultimately arrived at Duddeston Road, where during the usual wait I hunted around for a suitable bolt to insert between the upper edge of the baffle plate and the firehole mouth. Smoke baffles did not always fit too well and tended to drop down at the forward end, which in turn obstructed the free flight of coal from the shovel blade to the front of the grate. Having adjusted the baffle to my satisfaction, I built up the fire rather more than usual for a Bordesley, anticipating that we were going to have a struggle. Jack then climbed down and checked that the sanding gear was still functioning correctly by the time-honoured method of holding the back of his hand in front of the delivery pipe while I operated the valve.

At last our signal came off and Jack, having first given a prolonged crow on the whistle, opened both sand valve and regulator. We eased slowly forward, gradually gathering speed, but any attempt at vigorous acceleration resulted in a slip, and Jack had to coax her along very gently indeed. The distants were off for St.Andrews but, despite all his expertise with the regulator, it was pretty obvious by the time we had passed Landor Street box that we were not going to build up sufficient momentum to stand even half a chance of getting up the bank. 'We're not going to make it,' observed Jack resignedly as we thumped slowly past Brickyard crossing. Having come to the same conclusion some little while ago, I had left the firedoors wide open so as to allow the steam pressure to fall back, for we had more than we could use and I wanted to avoid blowing off as much as possible. She would not keep her feet even on full first valve, and now that we were on the 1 in 62 section what speed we had rapidly fell away. It was frustrating not being able to transmit the power available to the drawbar, but with such poor adhesion we had no other choice, and after a final violent slip we came to a standstill some fifty yards short of St.Andrew's signal box.

'I'm sure we've got a dickens of a lot more on than fifty,' said Jack, as I screwed the tender brake on as hard as possible. 'We should have come up better than that even though we were slipping,' he continued. I had not sufficient experience at that time to comment on the matter, but from my observations in the pilots we should have managed thirty wagons or so ourselves if the pilot was fully extended. After some ten minutes we saw a column of black smoke move up behind the feather

of white steam coming from our pilot's safety valves,
and seconds later clearly heard the shrill, distinctive
crow whistle indicating that both were ready. I quickly
released the hand brake while Jack hooted our reply and
then, after letting our engine roll back half a turn, he
heaved open the regulator to the full first valve.
There was a volcanic eruption from the chimney, the cab
rattled and shook, while the wheels churned showers of
sparks from the rails, but we did not move forward a
single inch. Jack tried again as I leaned out of my
window in an effort to see what the bankers were up to,
but twin pillars of smoke and steam left no doubt that
they were trying as hard as we were, and slipping just
as badly. Jack made several attempts, but it was of no
avail - the train might just as well have been welded to
the track.

'I'm going to have a word with the bobby to see what's
to be done,' said Jack, climbing down the steps after
the final abortive effort. Things must be bad if we
can't get moving with two bankers, I thought. Having
little to do but wait, I decided to see if I could
improve our traction by the old method of applying grit
to the rails. Leaving the steam brake on as a precaution, I descended shovel in hand to the ground and
foraged around for some suitable material. I soon found
what I was looking for in the form of a dark grey gravel
lying at the side of the track. Although much coarser
than sand, the chips were small enough for the purpose
in mind and would crush under the wheels to form an
abrasive layer. Scooping up a shovelful I quickly ran a
trail along the surfaces of both rails for a distance of
some fifty yards in front of our engine, and I had just
completed this operation when Jack returned from the box.
'They're running a train up behind the bankers,' he said,
'which will then give us a nudge to get us started.
Once on the move we should be O.K. with two pilots.' I
must admit that I had not seen this manoeuvre done
before, but it seemed sound reasoning and would cause
less delay than employing a third banking engine.

Once again the crow whistle could be clearly heard
from the rear and once again Jack heaved open the regulator. This time we moved forwards, did half a slip and
then moved forwards again. After a couple of laboured
revolutions Jack, taking heart from our new-found
adhesion, pushed the regulator up to the horizontal and
lo and behold we staggered on, gaining speed at every
beat. My treatment of the rail surfaces proved very

effective, for Jack was able to use both full gear and
regulator until we were well and truly underway. Our
exhaust crashed out in a deep-throated explosive roar
which was absolutely deafening as I leaned out and
regarded this unusual spectacle of an 8F heading fifty
wagons banked by two pilots, which were being pushed in
turn by a 4F hauling a train of some further forty
wagons assisted by yet another pilot. Once off the
gritted section we started to slip again but our speed
had built up sufficiently to enable Jack to come back to
the first valve which, with both pilots fully extended,
enabled us to claw our way slowly up to Bordesley Junction. Jack took it very steadily indeed on entering the
branch but even so it required the combined efforts of
the sanders and a bit of reverse gear to stop at the
signal. It was only after we had shunted out the train
that the true reason for our difficulties came to light,
and needless to say our guard was given a lengthy and
pointed lecture on the subject of loadings.

The Bordesleys, therefore, had their moments of
excitement, but in the main they were leisurely, mundane
affairs involving more talking than shovelling.

The following week I found myself working on the
Kingsbury branch, a place I had never been to before
but, like all new jobs, it proved quite interesting.
The line served the North Warwickshire collieries of
Wood End and Baddesley and, in addition to being steeply
graded, it was not in the best of condition. Spice was
added to this by the fact that one of the local drivers
had recently run away down the bank with a loaded coal
train. With commendable devotion to duty he had ordered
his mate to bale out while, remaining alone at the
controls, he had managed to attract the signalman's
attention with his frantic whistling. The runaway train
was then duly turned into an empty siding where it would
do least harm, but even so it ploughed into the stop-
block at a good rate of knots, reducing many of the
wagons to matchwood.

With this rather daunting prospect in mind I keenly
observed every section as we hauled our train of empties
up to Baddesley with 4F 3912. The job itself was
straightforward enough, involving a spot of shunting at
Kingsbury sidings before departing with the empty wagons
for the colliery. We worked tender-first up the bank to
Baddesley and this I found was a new experience, for I
could not recall having worked a train in reverse up an

incline before. Somehow the engine did not seem to
steam quite as well, although no doubt this was mainly
psychological, since the water level always showed a
pessimistic reading and one could not afford to mortgage
the boiler so much should the need arise.

At Baddesley we indulged in some more shunting in
order to make up our coal train, which was destined for
Washwood Heath Junction. However, before descending the
bank we had to have a certain proportion of the wagon
brakes pinned down in much the same manner as was practiced at the top of Bromsgrove bank, and whether one
kept the train successfully under control depended
largely on the guard's skill in assessing this
requirement accurately.

My speculations of a hair-raising run were quickly
dashed, for Jack had to literally drag the train fully
on to the incline before being able to shut off, and
then the hand brake alone was practically sufficient to
keep us in check until we arrived at Kingsbury once
again. Our journey to Washwood Heath was via the slow
line which took in Whitacre and Coleshill, and I welcomed the opportunity to familiarise myself with this
section, for there is no better way to learn a route
than from the footplate of a coal train. It was also
just a sufficiently long trip to get to know the ways of
a Class 4F and experiment with firing techniques without
the possibility of inviting too much trouble. I found
in due course that they were basically similar to Class
3s and responded in a more leisurely way to approximately
the same treatment, but being superheated they always
worked more efficiently when the elements had well and
truly warmed up. This warming-up period of course took
a certain amount of time and if serious work was to be
contemplated it paid to anticipate the event as much as
possible and keep the fire bright, even at the expense
of wasting steam through the safety valves.

Two weeks later I was introduced to another series of
places I had never been to before. These were along the
Walsall line from Castle Bromwich and in summer it
proved to be a delightfully pleasant run, since the
route involved journeying through the very picturesque
Sutton Park, where dense woods contrasted favourably
with Birmingham's industrial areas.

At Castle Bromwich the track curves in a long sweep
to the left on a low embankment where an excellent view
could be had of the airfield on one side and the sludge
treatment works on the other. At Park Lane signal box

the line merged with the one leading down into Water
Orton sidings, forming a triangle which was useful when
an engine required to be turned. From Park Lane the
line climbed at 1 in 157 over a bridge at Kingsbury Road,
through Walmley and past Wylde Green golf course up to
Sutton Coldfield, where a small goods yard lay on the
down side surrounded by trees - a very pleasant spot in
which to spend a leisurely half hour knocking out and
picking up the odd wagon or two. From the goods yard
the climb continued up through the woods of Sutton Park,
where holidaymakers could be seen enjoying themselves
boating on the well-known Bracebridge Pool. Just beyond
the park was Streetley station and, after passing Round-
about Wood, the line crossed the Chester road on a high
embankment before proceeding up to Aldridge sidings, the
summit of the bank. Our trip terminated at this point,
and after more shunting we returned to Water Orton with
usually a light train of freight, bound for northern
parts. As might be imagined, the work was not very
exacting and made no undue demands from either side of
the footplate, but in keeping with the majority of Trip
link jobs it afforded the opportunity to get to know
thoroughly all aspects of railway operations over that
section.
     After a further interlude of local work including
another Bordesley, we were booked on the Rubery trip,
our farthest journey west, and again this was interesting for me since it entailed breaking fresh ground once
more. Following the general pattern of most trip jobs,
loadings were not excessively heavy nor timings severe,
for after climbing the bank to Kings Heath we acted as a
pick-up until reaching Longbridge. Here was the site of
the well-known Austin Motor Works and the Halesowen
branch made its way between the massive blocks of that
extensive plant. The Austin works had its own sidings
and, for that matter, its own motive power in the form
of powerful 0-6-0 saddle tanks, painted in a distinctive
bright green livery and invariably immaculately turned
out. As may be imagined, a plant the size of Austins
daily required a great deal of material and also facilities for removing the unending flow from the assembly
lines. The sidings were, therefore, very busy indeed.
     On arrival, we quickly shunted out our train and,
while this was in progress, I was able to take note of
the intense activity all around. Longbridge sidings
was really in two parts, the section nearest to the
junction being devoted exclusively to works traffic,

whilst 200 yards farther along the line towards Rubery were some more tracks laid to serve the locality in general, in addition to Austins' overspill. Here also were the twin station platforms over which tramped the feet of countless workers brought in from not only the city but the dormitory towns lying to the west. Having done our duty at Longbridge, we proceeded the half-mile or so up a 1 in 96 gradient to Rubery, where after a further shunting session we took our lunch before returning to Lawley Street, picking up at intermediate sidings as required. It was an exceedingly pleasant little job, and terminating opposite the loco we were usually well placed for booking off at approximately the same time every day.

About this time in August 1952, a buff-coloured envelope bearing an 'Official Paid' stamp was waiting for me on the hall table when I returned home from work. With mixed feelings I hastily tore open the flap and read the contents. It contained a brief letter requesting me to report to Aldershot, a travel warrant to facilitate this, and some instructions regarding what to take, which incidentally was very little.

I felt relief that the long wait and uncertainties were now over, but on the other hand the inevitable butterflies of not knowing quite what was in store for me over the next two years. My brother had related details of life in the army, and I must admit that some of the restrictions and severe discipline, not to mention other aspects such as lack of home comforts and leisure, held little appeal. However, I was resolved to make the best of matters and try and gain as much as I could from the experience.

In August 1954, after my service in the R.A.S.C. - principally in Germany - the long-awaited day of my demobilisation arrived. Two years to the day I re-entered civilian life. I had learned many new things during this time, to drive, to shoot, to receive and give orders, but most important perhaps the ability to live in harmony with my fellow men. The army also taught me to appreciate all the things we normally take for granted in this materialistic age; one's home, good food and freedom of choice - a diminishing commodity nowadays, but precious nevertheless.

Despite familiar faces and unchanged surrounds, I felt rather like a stranger when I visited the loco for the first time to advise them that I was once more

available. Until a place could be found for me in the
bottom road group to which my seniority now entitled me,
I was placed in the Control link.

Things had changed only in a few details, with the
exception of the proposed staff amenity block. I also
saw for the first time one of the new B.R. Standard
Class 5s, which on the whole appealed to me aesthetic-
ally from most angles, and ergonomically I thought the
footplate layout was a vast improvement on anything yet
built. I was still, of course, at this stage trying to
readjust to civilian life, but it was remarkable how
quickly I slipped into the swing of things again.

At the end of two weeks, involving a variety of local
jobs, I felt almost as though I had never had a two year
break, and even my muscles had ceased to ache and my
hands were regaining their former toughness. On the
Saturday of the second week, the foreman called my
attention to the roster board, where he pointed out with
a friendly smile that I was now booked with driver Syd
Lloyd in Link Three section C. 'Syd Lloyd?' I queried.
'What's he like?' 'Oh, he's a great chap,' replied the
foreman enthusiastically. 'A real character. You'll get
on fine with him, without a doubt.'

Well, I would soon find out, for we were to work the
8.45 p.m. Gloucester from the West End, booking on at
7.16 to prepare our own engine. I went home that night
feeling for the first time that I could now be considered an experienced fireman, and looking forward very
much indeed to next week's work.

The sequel to this volume by T.R.Essery is entitled
MORE FIRING DAYS AT SALTLEY
and continues the story of his rise through the links
as fireman during the remainder of his career on
British Railways, including his experiences on the 'Carlisles' and
epic runs on these with stoker-fitted 9Fs. The author was not
only an exceptional footplateman in his skill and dedication
but has the ability to tell his story in a way
that has seldom, if ever, been equalled